QUINN TAYLOR

Red Flag Radar

Spot problematic behaviors early when online dating

Copyright © 2025 by Quinn Taylor

All rights reserved. No part of this publication may be reproduced, stored or transmitted in any form or by any means, electronic, mechanical, photocopying, recording, scanning, or otherwise without written permission from the publisher. It is illegal to copy this book, post it to a website, or distribute it by any other means without permission.

Quinn Taylor asserts the moral right to be identified as the author of this work.

Quinn Taylor has no responsibility for the persistence or accuracy of URLs for external or third-party Internet Websites referred to in this publication and does not guarantee that any content on such Websites is, or will remain, accurate or appropriate.

Designations used by companies to distinguish their products are often claimed as trademarks. All brand names and product names used in this book and on its cover are trade names, service marks, trademarks and registered trademarks of their respective owners. The publishers and the book are not associated with any product or vendor mentioned in this book. None of the companies referenced within the book have endorsed the book.

First edition

This book was professionally typeset on Reedsy.
Find out more at reedsy.com

Contents

Introduction · 1

I Part One

1. The Changing Landscape of Dating · 9
2. The Toxic Relationship Cycle · 13
3. Common Problematic Behaviors · 23
4. Red Flag Behaviors on Social Media · 42
5. Personality Disorders and Associated Behaviors · 46
6. Making Sense of the Toxic Relationship Cycle and Behaviors · 56
7. Recognizing Patterns and Protecting Yourself · 66

II Part Two

8. Setting Boundaries and Protecting Yourself · 73
9. Building Healthy Relationships · 83
10. Moving Forward with Confidence · 88
11. Reference · 92

III BONUS CHAPTER

12. The Special Case of Long-Distance Relationships · 95

Introduction

The Promise of Online Dating

Online dating has revolutionized how people connect, offering an unparalleled opportunity to meet potential partners beyond traditional social and geographical boundaries. It provides a platform to discover individuals with shared interests, values, and goals, enabling connections that might never have occurred otherwise. Whether seeking casual companionship, meaningful relationships, or long-term love, online dating allows greater control over the romantic journey in ways that were unimaginable just a few decades ago.

The flexibility of these platforms caters to diverse lifestyles, giving busy professionals, single parents, or those in remote locations the chance to meet others on their own terms. Beyond romantic relationships, some even find valuable friendships or networks through the process. Online dating also encourages a deeper understanding of personal relationship needs, allowing for the refinement of preferences regarding interests, values, or life goals. For many, the experience offers both the potential for connection and valuable self-discovery.

Challenges in the Digital Dating World

However, online dating is not without its challenges. The abundance of profiles can feel overwhelming, making it difficult to separate genuine connections from superficial interactions. Many users present highly curated versions of themselves, which can blur the lines between authenticity and performance. The fast-paced nature of swiping and matching often prioritizes instant attraction over meaningful compatibility. Furthermore, the anonymity of online platforms sometimes emboldens manipulative or harmful behaviors, highlighting the importance of approaching online dating with both hope and caution.

Who this Book is For

This book is designed for those embarking on an online dating journey, eager to explore new connections while remaining mindful of potential pitfalls. It is also for individuals in the early stages of a relationship who have begun noticing behaviors that create unease, such as emotional inconsistency or boundary violations. Additionally, it serves anyone concerned about a loved one who might be entangled in a relationship that appears to be eroding their emotional well-being. By offering clarity, tools, and practical strategies, this book aims to help readers recognize problematic behaviors early, protect their mental health, and build connections based on mutual respect and understanding.

The Emotional and Psychological Cost of Problematic Behaviors in Relationships

Harmful relationship patterns can significantly affect emotional and psychological well-being. They often erode self-esteem, create confusion, and foster unhealthy dependency, making it difficult to break free. Manipulation, controlling tendencies, and emotional instability frequently contribute to anxiety, depression, and a sense of worthlessness.

The effects of toxic relationships do not always end when the relationship does. Many individuals subsequently struggle with trusting others, forming healthy attachments, and feeling secure in future partnerships. Recognizing troubling patterns early provides an opportunity to safeguard emotional health and avoid the lasting consequences of entanglement in toxic dynamics.

Limitations of this Book

This book offers guidance on identifying problematic behaviors and protecting emotional well-being but does not replace professional mental health support. Every relationship and personal history is unique, and more complex issues related to past trauma, personality disorders, or abusive dynamics may require the assistance of a qualified therapist or counselor. The goal here is to raise awareness and provide practical tools, not to serve as a diagnostic or therapeutic manual.

Additionally, the primary focus is on early intervention and prevention rather than recovery from long-term abusive relationships. Those who have experienced prolonged toxic relationships may need specialized resources and professional guidance well beyond what is covered in these pages. If this is your situation, then this book can help with context, but you should seek support from mental health professionals and those in your personal network that you trust.

Structure of the Book

Part 1 - Tuning Your Red Flag Radar

The first part of this book examines the evolving landscape of online dating, including the role of anonymity and the ways in which digital interactions can enable both meaningful connections and deceptive behaviors. It explores the reasons problematic behaviors flourish online and how the nature of these platforms can create an environment where manipulation and dishonesty thrive.

A closer look is then taken at the toxic relationship cycle, which includes phases of idealization, devaluation, and discard. This pattern explains how some individuals initially appear perfect, showering their partners with attention and affection, only to later shift toward criticism, emotional manipulation, and eventual rejection. Indeed, if you are unfortunate enough to meet someone online dating who is inauthentic and begins to exhibit problematic behaviors, then any relationship you enter will probably follow a surprisingly predictable trajectory. Recognizing this cycle early is crucial to avoiding harmful entanglements.

Problematic behaviors that frequently arise as a part of the toxic relationship cycle are examined next. This includes manipulative tactics such as gaslighting, emotional withdrawal, and coercion, providing a deeper understanding of the signs that may indicate an unhealthy dynamic. Following this, attention is turned to online red flag behaviors that are particularly prevalent on social media, where digital communication often amplifies deception, impulsivity, and boundary violations.

A dedicated section provides insight into personality disorders and associated behaviors. Some harmful relationship patterns may stem from conditions such as narcissistic personality disorder or borderline personality disorder, though not all problematic behaviors arise from a diagnosable disorder. Many behaviors can also be rooted in past traumas, unmet emotional needs, or learned relational patterns. This section is included to offer awareness and insight into these conditions, providing context and empowerment rather than encouraging diagnosis. Keep in mind that the primary goal is to recognize behaviors that undermine emotional well-being, regardless of their underlying cause.

The final chapters of this section focuses on making sense of toxic behaviors, whether they are conscious or unconscious, and the dangers of trauma bonding. Guidance is provided on recognizing when it is time to leave a harmful situation and how to exit safely. A deeper exploration of recurring patterns ensures the development of strategies to safeguard emotional well-being.

INTRODUCTION

Part 2 – Dating Well

The second part of the book shifts focus to proactive strategies for dating well. The importance of setting and enforcing boundaries is emphasized, with practical guidance on how to communicate limits effectively to prevent entanglement with individuals who may seek to manipulate or control.

Finally, the characteristics of a healthy relationship are explored, defining the elements of a secure, mutually respectful partnership. This might feel incredibly obvious, but just because it is obvious, it does not make it trivial. By recognizing the contrast between toxic and healthy dynamics, informed choices can be made about where to invest time and emotional energy. Understanding these distinctions provides greater confidence in navigating the dating world while maintaining emotional resilience and self-respect.

Empowerment Through Awareness

Ultimately his book is centered on empowerment, recognizing what feels right, addressing what does not, and making decisions that prioritize emotional well-being. The objective is not to vilify anyone who might have a personality disorder, or indeed encourage an attempt at diagnosis. The aim is to highlight behaviors that can negatively impact relationships and your emotional health. Whether seeking love, navigating a new relationship, or supporting someone else, the knowledge and tools provided here aim to bring clarity, confidence, and self-respect to the dating experience.

So, let's make a start. The first chapter explores why problematic behaviors are so common in online dating and how to approach the opportunities and challenges with confidence.

I

Part One

Tuning Your Red Flag Radar

1

The Changing Landscape of Dating

Online dating has revolutionized the way we search for love and companionship, offering possibilities that were unimaginable just a few decades ago. With a few taps on a screen, you can access a vast pool of potential matches, transcending geographical boundaries and introducing you to people you might never have met otherwise. For those embarking on this journey, it can feel exciting, hopeful, and full of potential. Yet, for all its promise, online dating also brings unique challenges that require awareness and discernment.

For those in the early stages of a relationship, the initial thrill of connection can sometimes be tempered by nagging doubts or concerning behaviors. Is this relationship healthy? Are these quirks just minor flaws, or do they signal deeper issues? Whether you're swiping through profiles or navigating a budding relationship, this chapter is designed to help you understand the new dynamics of modern dating and begin to equip you with tools to recognize healthy and problematic patterns.

The Rise of Online Dating

In the past, meeting a potential partner often relied on proximity. People connected through shared communities, workplaces, or introductions from friends and family. These settings provided a level of accountability and context where mutual acquaintances could vouch for someone's character and intentions. While limited in scope, these traditional methods offered a degree of built-in reassurance.

Online dating has removed many of these constraints, allowing individuals to connect across cities, countries, and even continents. Platforms like Tinder, Bumble, and Hinge make it possible to meet people outside of your immediate social circle, while services like eHarmony and Match promise compatibility through sophisticated algorithms. For introverts or those with busy lives, these platforms can feel like a lifeline, offering opportunities to connect without the pressures of traditional social settings.

However, the benefits of online dating come with a new set of challenges. The sheer volume of options can lead to decision fatigue, making it harder to focus on meaningful connections. Additionally, the anonymity of these platforms allows users to present curated versions of themselves, which may not always align with reality.

The Anonymity Factor

One of the most significant shifts in modern dating is the role of anonymity. Unlike traditional settings, where shared networks or mutual friends could provide context about a person's background and intentions, online dating often operates in a vacuum. This lack of external accountability makes it easier for individuals to manipulate, mislead, or exploit others.

For example, a charming profile might not be what it seems. It might mask more profound issues, such as emotional unavailability or a tendency for manipulation that you simply cannot spot in the vacuum of online dating. Initial conversations can feel thrilling, but without a shared community or context, it's harder to verify someone's authenticity. This is why many people describe online dating as both exhilarating and risky; the potential for connection is high, but so is the potential for misrepresentation.

Why Problematic Behaviors Flourish Online

The structure of online dating platforms can inadvertently create an environment where problematic behaviors thrive. Here are some reasons why:

- **Superficiality:** Swiping through profiles encourages quick judgments based on appearance or surface-level information. This focus on superficial traits can result in you missing opportunities where deeper compatibility is possible. The opposite is also true, where you can be drawn into a charismatic profile where the images might feed your fantasy but where there is no true compatibility. If a match is made, it can lead to a highly inauthentic connection where what both parties say and do isn't consistent with what they know, think, and feel.
- **Validation-Seeking:** Some users prioritize gaining matches and attention over forming genuine connections, which can lead to later behaviors offline like love bombing followed by ghosting.
- **An Abundance of Options:** The seemingly endless stream of potential matches fosters a "grass is always greener" mentality, making it harder for some to commit or take relationships seriously. Why settle for someone who is a few centimeters shorter than your ideal if the perfect match might be on the following profile?
- **Anonymity:** The ability to disengage without consequences emboldens some individuals to act dishonestly or disrespectfully. This often manifests in the widespread behavior of creating dating profiles that are misleading. Misrepresentations can occur on

almost any dimension, from using photographs decades old to incorrect age statements and flat-out lies regarding marital status. Inaccurate profiles can tell you a lot about the person you are connecting with, and they should elicit varying levels of concern on your part. For example, if they say they are 39 years old when, in fact, they turn out to be 44, then you can surmise they are not confident in who they are today. If they say they are single when they are married, then you can conclude they are downright manipulative.

Staying Grounded

None of this is insurmountable, but it does highlight the importance of approaching online dating cautiously and intentionally. Finding a fulfilling connection online is possible, but it is just as likely that you won't. With so many factors at play, including superficial interactions, anonymity, and the constant lure of something better, dating apps create an environment where problematic behaviors can thrive. This does not mean you should give up on dating, but it does mean you need to approach it with clarity. The best way to protect yourself is to recognize the early warning signs of unhealthy dynamics before you get pulled in. And that starts with understanding the toxic relationship cycle.

2

The Toxic Relationship Cycle

Toxic relationships rarely start with glaring red flags. Instead, they often begin with intense passion, affection, and charm, qualities that make it easy to overlook initial warning signs. Problem behaviors, such as love bombing, gaslighting, excessive jealousy, and others, don't all show up at once. Instead, they emerge at different stages of the toxic relationship, forming a surprisingly predictable cycle that is as damaging as it is difficult to escape. For those exploring online dating or in the early stages of a relationship, a good level of awareness of this cycle will help you protect yourself from getting into a damaging relationship and the long-term emotional harm that might result.

The Three Phases of the Toxic Cycle

The toxic relationship cycle typically consists of three distinct phases: idealization, devaluation, and discard. Each phase brings its own set of behaviors, drawing you in, breaking you down, and leaving you questioning everything. Here is how to recognize these phases:

The Idealization Phase: A Bond that Feels Unbreakable

Every toxic relationship begins with a dream, an exhilarating whirlwind where everything feels perfect. This is the idealization phase, where your partner creates an illusion so compelling it feels like destiny. Through love bombing and sex bombing, they overwhelm you with affection, attention, and grand gestures. They declare you their soulmate, share bold visions of your future together, and accelerate the pace of the relationship, making it feel like a connection that was meant to be. Physical intimacy often happens quickly, strengthening the emotional connection and creating a bond that feels impossible to break.

Mirroring plays a key role during this phase. They reflect your interests, values, and even your quirks, making you feel deeply understood, as if you've found someone who truly "gets" you. Occasionally, you might feel a sense of unease, moments where their responses feel overly rehearsed or strangely aligned with your own thoughts. But you brush it off because the connection feels so right, so easy, and so rare.

As part of this intensity, they begin asking deep and probing questions about your past relationships, often couched in empathy. They seem eager to understand your experiences, your hurts, and what went wrong before. Their questions feel disarmingly kind, as though they genuinely care about what you've been through. What you don't realize, though, is that this information is being stored, ready to be weaponized against you later. Stories of past heartbreak, insecurities, or vulnerabilities will eventually be used to manipulate or control you, often in ways you couldn't anticipate at this stage.

Amidst the euphoria, subtle red flags begin to emerge. They might start testing your boundaries in small, seemingly romantic ways. For example, they may call you late at night, keep the conversation going for hours, and suggest it's cute or special when you both fall asleep together on the phone. They may push for deeply personal details about your life far earlier than feels natural or want to spend every waking moment together, framing it as intense love. At first, these behaviors seem flattering or exciting, but they reveal an unhealthy tendency to overstep boundaries, setting the stage for more significant intrusions down the line.

This phase is intoxicating, and losing yourself in it is easy. The speed of the relationship, the constant attention, and their apparent vulnerability draw you in. You may find yourself actively contributing to the whirlwind, opening up more than you typically would, sharing secrets, or staying on those late-night calls because it all feels so special. There's a sense of mutual culpability here: you're swept up in the romance, even though part of you may sense things are moving too fast. But it's nearly impossible to slow down because the connection feels so good, and you don't want to lose it.

It's crucial to understand that this stage is not what it seems. The behaviors that feel romantic, love bombing, mirroring, probing into your past, and so on, are calculated to foster dependency and bypass your instincts. They draw you into a bond that feels irreplaceable, while those minor boundary-pushing behaviors and probing questions plant the seeds for future manipulation.

By the time the cracks in this idealization phase start to show, you're already deeply emotionally invested. The bond feels so strong that walking away seems unthinkable. This is the power of the idealization phase: it creates an emotional high so addictive that you overlook the warning signs. Healthy relationships take time to build, with trust and respect growing gradually. If things feel too good to be true, it's worth stepping back and asking whether this connection is built on genuine trust or an illusion crafted to ensnare you.

The Devaluation Phase: The Erosion of Trust

As the intoxicating high of the idealization phase fades, so does their charm. The person who once made you feel like the center of their world begins to shift. Subtle criticisms start to creep into daily interactions. What they once adored about you, your independence, humor, or ambition, now becomes a source of irritation. Your independence might now be labeled selfishness, your humor deemed immature, and your ambition criticized for neglecting their needs. Over time, these criticisms escalate, making you feel you're constantly falling short of their expectations.

The devaluation phase might start gradually, with minor remarks and subtle changes in behavior, or it might begin suddenly and unexpectedly, triggered by something you consider entirely innocent. For instance, you might bump into an old acquaintance of the opposite sex, greet them warmly, and think nothing of it, only to be met with an astonishing level of jealous rage as soon as they are no longer present. Suddenly, you're accused of being overly familiar, disrespectful, or even unfaithful. Caught off guard, you find yourself justifying, arguing, explaining, and denying. The irony is that the more you defend yourself, the more power you hand over to them as they gain control over your emotions and actions.

Gaslighting becomes a key tactic during this phase, making you doubt your perceptions and instincts. They may deny having said something hurtful, accuse you of overreacting, or claim you're imagining things. For example, they might deny ever being critical of you, even when you vividly remember the conversation, or accuse you of being *"too emotional"* when you respond to their cutting remarks. Their behavior becomes unpredictable. One day, they're affectionate and apologetic. The next day, cold, distant, or openly hostile. This inconsistency keeps you in a state of confusion as you try to regain the harmony you once had.

Love withdrawal also surfaces as a cruel form of control. They may withhold affection, attention, or intimacy as punishment, leaving you desperate for their approval. When you try to confront them, they might engage in stonewalling, refusing to address your concerns, dismissing them as overreactions, or accusing you of being too needy. These invalidating tactics slowly chip away at your confidence and sense of self-worth.

Other manipulative behaviors, like triangulation, emerge. They may compare you unfavorably to an ex, a friend, or even a stranger, saying things like, *"My ex would never have acted this way,"* or *"Why can't you be more like so-and-so?"* These comparisons are designed to make you feel inadequate, fuelling your need to win back their approval. Simultaneously, excessive jealousy and control begin to take hold. They might monitor your actions, falsely accuse you of infidelity, or dictate how you should behave, all while framing their behavior as concern or love.

Financial manipulation may also appear. They might control shared resources, guilt you into covering expenses, or criticize your financial decisions. At the same time, they might show indifference to your successes, failing to celebrate your achievements or diminishing them entirely. No matter how hard you try or how much you give, it feels like nothing is ever good enough.

The devaluation phase is difficult to escape because it isn't all bad. There are just enough good days to keep you stuck: weekend trips away, movie nights, walks in the countryside, or romantic dinners, where everything seems to return to "normal." These fleeting moments of kindness and affection echo the idealization phase to which you hope to return. They make you believe that the person you fell for is still there, and if you just try a little harder, things will return to the way they were.

But this cycle of brief highs and crushing lows is deliberate. By giving you glimpses of the relationship you're desperately trying to save, they deepen your emotional dependence and ensure you stay invested. The longer this phase continues, the more your confidence, sense of self-worth, and emotional security erode.

This phase marks a dangerous turning point. The person you adored now feels unreachable, yet you remain, hoping to recapture the connection you once had. But the truth is, the more you justify, explain, and argue, the more control they gain. The devaluation phase is not an anomaly; it's a pattern that traps you in confusion and harm. Without intervention, the relationship will unlikely improve and only deteriorate.

The Discard Phase: The Final Blow (Or is it?)

Eventually, the relationship reaches a breaking point. The person who once seemed so devoted now feels like a stranger. They begin to pull away, either emotionally or physically, leaving you feeling abandoned, confused, and emotionally wrecked. This phase might come suddenly without warning, as they ghost you without explanation. One day, they're there; the next, they're gone. While devastating, this abrupt end can sometimes be a blessing in disguise: it may be the easiest way to escape the toxic cycle.

More often, however, the discard phase is not so clean. Toxic partners rarely leave quietly. Instead, they orchestrate their exit with dramatic accusations designed to destabilize and hurt you further. They might say, *"You never really loved me,"* or *"I gave you everything, and you gave me nothing,"* flipping the blame onto you. Alternatively, they might position themselves as the victim, saying things like, *"I've never been treated so badly in my life,"* or *"I don't understand why I'm not good enough."* These statements are calculated to provoke guilt, defensiveness, and confusion, pulling you into yet another cycle of justifying yourself, explaining your actions, and even begging them to stay. Your responses to their emotional manipulation hand them even more power, allowing them to dictate the terms of the relationship even as they prepare to leave.

During the discard phase, false accusations often intensify. They might accuse you of infidelity, selfishness, or being the reason for their unhappiness. These claims are designed to keep you off balance and questioning your own worth. For example, they might suddenly declare, *"You've been cheating on me all along, haven't you?"* even when there's no basis for the accusation. These unfounded attacks are not about seeking the truth; they're about control and inflicting emotional harm.

Another hallmark of the discard phase is triangulation. Toxic partners often already have someone else lined up before they leave and may not be shy about letting you know. They might say something cruel like, *"At least someone else will appreciate me,"* or deliberately flaunt their new partner to deepen your sense of betrayal. The knowledge that they've moved on so quickly can leave you reeling, as it seems to invalidate everything you thought you shared.

Financial manipulation may also come to a head during this stage. They might demand repayment for things they once freely gave or refuse to settle shared debts, leaving you financially burdened and emotionally depleted. This tactic ensures their hold on you extends even after they've gone, tying you to the relationship through lingering obligations or disputes.

And yet, the discard isn't always permanent. Toxic partners, particularly narcissists, often reappear after a period of absence. This is commonly known as "hoovering." They might claim to miss you, profess regret, or insist they've changed, reigniting the hope of returning to the magical beginning. This rekindling often mimics the idealization phase, but it is a watered-down version. It is less intense, shorter-lasting, and with diminishing returns. For example, they might reach out with a simple text saying, *"I miss us,"* or a nostalgic mention of a shared memory to pull you back in. But this isn't love; it's manipulation, designed to keep you tethered to the cycle.

Throughout this phase, the toxic partner continues to test boundaries.

They might reappear just as you begin to move on, destabilizing your progress. The promise of returning to the early days, when everything felt perfect, is seductive but ultimately an illusion. Each return leaves you more depleted, more demoralized, and further from the life and emotional stability you deserve.

The discard phase represents the end of the toxic cycle. It's devastating, confusing, and emotionally exhausting, yet it's also an opportunity to break free. Recognizing the patterns, emotional manipulation, blame-shifting, triangulation, false accusations, and financial control is crucial to resisting their attempts to re-enter your life. The cycle only continues if you allow it.

The Irony of Accommodation

In toxic relationships, the harder you try to meet your partner's expectations, keep the peace, or salvage what feels like a relationship worth fighting for, the more unbalanced the dynamic becomes. Acts of compromise, which may initially seem like loving gestures, often evolve into patterns of self-abandonment. Over time, you find yourself sacrificing your own needs, boundaries, and sense of self in the hope of making things work.

It often begins innocently enough: canceling plans with friends to prioritize their desires, adjusting your schedule to fit theirs, or holding back your feelings to avoid conflict. These small sacrifices can feel reasonable at first, but they escalate. Gradually, you stop prioritizing what matters to you, focusing entirely on their wants and expectations. You begin giving up pieces of yourself to maintain the relationship without realizing it.

The cruel paradox is that this willingness to accommodate rarely earns the respect or appreciation you hope for. Instead, it often fuels their contempt. Toxic partners may interpret your self-sacrifice as a sign of weakness or a lack of self-respect. They notice how far you'll bend to please them, and rather than valuing your effort, they use it against you. They might say things like, *"I lost respect for you a long time ago because you don't stand up for yourself,"* or criticize you for *"trying too hard."* These cutting remarks leave you drained, demoralized, and wondering why your efforts are never enough.

Even more damaging, this self-sacrifice cycle reinforces the relationship's power imbalance. You give them more control whenever you put their needs above your own. You might convince yourself that things will get better if you just try harder, give more, or change something about yourself. You hold onto the hope that your efforts will rekindle the connection you had in the beginning. But this hope is a mirage. Instead of restoring balance, your sacrifices pull you further into a cycle where your emotional needs are consistently sidelined.

This dynamic is exhausting because it creates the constant feeling of falling short. No matter how much you give, they demand more. Their shifting expectations and unpredictable behavior keep you striving for a standard that can never be met. Meanwhile, they remain firmly in control, dictating the terms of the relationship while you deplete yourself trying to meet them.

The irony of accommodation is that what you believe is saving the relationship often undermines it. You reinforce the imbalance that defines a toxic dynamic by consistently putting their needs first. In a healthy relationship, compromise is mutual and respectful. But in a toxic one, it's one-sided, leaving you disconnected from your own needs and boundaries.

Recognizing this irony is a vital step toward reclaiming your self-respect. Your willingness to accommodate reflects your care and commitment, not your failure. But to truly heal, you must prioritize your well-being over the impossible task of fixing something that cannot be fixed alone.

Recognizing the Cycle Early

The toxic relationship cycle often becomes most apparent in hindsight, but there are warning signs that can help you identify it early. Paying attention to these behaviors can save you from more profound emotional harm:

- **Rapid intensity**: While declarations of love, grand gestures, or talk of a future together within weeks of meeting may feel flattering, they are often red flags. A whirlwind pace can bypass your instincts and boundaries.
- **Sudden shifts**: Watch for abrupt changes from affection to criticism or withdrawal. This push-and-pull dynamic is destabilizing and designed to keep you striving for their approval.
- **Boundary violations**: Repeatedly ignoring or disrespecting your boundaries (emotional, physical, or social) is a key indicator of trouble. Healthy relationships respect personal limits.
- **Isolation tactics**: Attempts to discourage or sabotage your relationships with friends and family may initially seem subtle but often escalate. Isolation strengthens their control over you.

Recognizing these patterns early can help you protect yourself and avoid becoming trapped in the toxic cycle. Trust your instincts, set boundaries, and prioritize connections with supportive people. Now, let's take a look at some of the specific behaviours more deeply.

3

Common Problematic Behaviors

The previous chapter outlined how problematic relationships often unfold in distinct phases. In this section, we'll examine 26 specific red flag behaviors to be mindful of. Think of this as an opportunity to properly get your **red flag radar** tuned in so you can spot these patterns early. These behaviors are presented in a loose order that reflects how they may emerge over the course of a relationship, starting with subtle indicators and building toward more overt, harmful patterns. By paying attention to these signs, you can make informed decisions to safeguard your emotional health, whether setting boundaries, addressing concerns, or choosing to walk away from the relationship altogether.

1. Love Bombing

Love bombing sets the stage for a toxic relationship by overwhelming you with affection, compliments, and grand gestures. Imagine meeting someone who tells you within days that you're their soulmate, their twin flame, talks about future plans like marriage or starting a family, and showers you with extravagant gifts or constant attention. They might send you dozens of messages a day or surprise you with lavish dates that feel more like grand performances. While it might feel romantic and exciting, the intensity can feel disproportionate to the length of time you've known each other. This creates a fast emotional bond that makes it hard to step back and assess the relationship objectively. Love bombing often paves the way for control because the intense attachment makes you less likely to question their behavior later. If you find yourself feeling swept off your feet but overwhelmed, it's a signal to slow down and evaluate whether the relationship's pace aligns with your comfort level.

2. Sex Bombing

Following the intense affection of love bombing, sex bombing often accelerates emotional dependency. Physical intimacy may be introduced quickly, with your partner pushing for closeness that feels premature. They might insist on spending every night together, pressure you to move in quickly, or blur the lines between emotional and physical intimacy. For instance, they might frame physical closeness as proof of your love or as a way to "solidify" your bond. While chemistry is a natural and wonderful part of relationships, sex bombing accelerates this process, bypassing the emotional groundwork necessary for trust. If you notice intimacy being used to overshadow other issues or move the relationship forward at an unnatural pace, it's worth pausing to consider whether this dynamic feels right for you. Healthy intimacy evolves at a mutually comfortable pace.

3. Excessive Need for Validation

A partner who constantly seeks validation might seem vulnerable or endearing initially, but it can quickly become draining. They might frequently ask, *"Do you really love me?"* or demand reassurance about their worth, even in moments where it feels unwarranted. For example, they might repeatedly seek compliments on their appearance or question whether you find them attractive. This behavior often stems from deep insecurity, creating a dynamic where their emotional needs dominate the relationship. Over time, this neediness can make it difficult to address your own needs as their insecurities take center stage. It's important to recognize when this dynamic shifts from supportive to one-sided. While it's natural to reassure a partner occasionally, a constant demand for validation can stifle the natural reciprocity of a healthy partnership, leaving you feeling emotionally exhausted.

4. Mirroring

Mirroring occurs when your partner adopts your interests, hobbies, or values to create the illusion of compatibility. At first, this behavior can feel flattering and affirming, as though they truly understand you. For example, you might mention your love of a niche music genre, only to find them claiming an equally deep enthusiasm despite having no prior interest. Or perhaps you share an obscure passion for a particular book series, and they suddenly become an "expert" overnight. While it might seem sweet, excessive or overly specific mirroring can be a red flag, especially if it feels calculated rather than genuine.

Consider another scenario: early in the relationship, you might share that you have a positive relationship with an ex-partner. Perhaps it's someone you dated at university 20 years ago, and though the romantic connection ended long ago, you still communicate occasionally. Boundaries are in place, and they are now happily married. Your new partner might respond by mirroring this dynamic, claiming they, too, have amicable relationships with past partners. It seems like a reassuring sign that they're emotionally mature.

But as the relationship progresses, cracks begin to show. What initially seemed like shared values takes a darker turn. When you mention your positive connection with your ex again, your partner reacts with jealousy and rage. It becomes clear that their earlier claim wasn't true; they don't have good relationships with past partners and are consumed with insecurities and unresolved feelings about their own history. This sudden shift creates confusion and leaves you questioning their authenticity.

The psychology behind mirroring is about building trust quickly by making you feel seen and understood. But when mirroring lacks authenticity, it may indicate manipulation rather than genuine connection. A partner who mirrors excessively might prioritize creating emotional dependence over fostering a relationship rooted in mutual understanding and respect.

In healthy relationships, shared interests and values emerge naturally over time. While it's normal for partners to influence each other in positive ways, authentic connections are built on honesty, not on the illusion of compatibility created by mirroring. If you notice patterns of mirroring paired with inconsistency or dishonesty, it's worth reevaluating the relationship. Genuine compatibility doesn't require pretense; it thrives on transparency and mutual respect.

5. Exploitation of Vulnerabilities

Exploitation of vulnerabilities can feel particularly insidious because it often starts with what appears to be genuine interest and empathy. In the early days of the relationship, your partner may ask thoughtful, probing questions about your childhood, past relationships, or personal struggles. They may seem deeply invested in understanding you, which can create a sense of connection and trust. For example, you might share a story about a difficult breakup, only for it to resurface later as ammunition during an argument. They might say, *"After what you've been through, I thought you'd understand me better,"* or *"You're just projecting your past issues onto us,"* or *"Now I understand why your last two partners left you."* Over time, this tactic creates an emotional trap where the very things you confided in them are weaponized to control or manipulate you.

This form of manipulation leaves you feeling exposed and betrayed. It undermines your ability to trust not just your partner but others in the future. The exploitation of vulnerabilities often fosters a deep sense of dependency, as you begin to believe that no one else will ever understand or accept you the way they seem to. Recognizing this pattern is crucial for regaining control over your emotional well-being and rebuilding healthy boundaries.

6. Boundary Overstepping

Boundary overstepping often begins with small, seemingly innocuous actions that escalate over time. Early on, a partner might ask to read a text message *"just this once"* or insist on accompanying you to events where they weren't invited. While these gestures can be framed as signs of care or interest, they often signal a disregard for your personal boundaries. For instance, they might show up unannounced at your home or workplace, claiming they just *"missed you."* Another example is when they demand you share the passwords of your social media accounts, your internet banking account, and, indeed, any internet site you happen to visit.

Over time, these behaviors can grow more intrusive, leaving you feeling as though you have no space that's truly your own. A partner who consistently disregards your boundaries is unlikely to respect your autonomy, which is essential for a healthy relationship. Recognizing these small oversteps early on allows you to assert your limits before the pattern becomes ingrained.

7. Unrealistic Expectations

A partner with unrealistic expectations often sets a standard that feels impossible to meet. They might expect you to anticipate their needs without communication or fulfill roles that extend far beyond a healthy partnership. For example, they might say, *"If you really loved me, you'd know what I need,"* or *"You're the only one who truly understands me,"* placing immense pressure on you to be their sole source of support.

This dynamic creates an environment where you're constantly striving for approval, only to fall short of their unspoken expectations. Over time, these unrealistic demands can lead to feelings of inadequacy and exhaustion. A healthy relationship involves mutual effort and understanding, not one-sided expectations that leave you drained.

8. Over-Reliance on Sob Stories

While sharing personal struggles is a natural part of building intimacy, over-reliance on sob stories can become a tool for manipulation. A partner might frequently bring up their hardships to elicit sympathy, deflect accountability, or justify their behavior. For instance, they might say, *"You know how hard my childhood was,"* as an excuse for their lack of communication or poor treatment of you.

This behavior creates an imbalance where their needs and emotions consistently overshadow yours. While empathy is important, it's equally important to recognize when vulnerability is being used as a means of control. A healthy relationship balances mutual support without making one partner feel solely responsible for the other's emotional well-being.

9. Blame-Shifting

Blame-shifting emerges as conflicts arise, turning accountability into an elusive goal. When confronted about hurtful behavior, they might deflect with statements like, *"If you hadn't done [that], I wouldn't have reacted this way,"* or *"You're the reason I act like this."* This tactic shifts focus away from their actions, making you feel responsible for the relationship's problems. For example, if they lash out during an argument, they might justify their behavior by pointing to something you said weeks ago. Over time, this pattern erodes your confidence in addressing issues openly, as every conversation becomes about your perceived shortcomings. Blame-shifting prevents resolution and reinforces an unbalanced dynamic where their needs and actions dominate, leaving you constantly on the defensive.

10. Gaslighting

Gaslighting is a deliberate and insidious tactic designed to make you doubt your perceptions, memories, or feelings. It often begins subtly but escalates into a systematic erosion of your confidence in your own reality. For instance, a gaslighting partner might deny things they've said or done, even when you have clear recollections or evidence. They may tell you, *"You're imagining things,"* or *"You're being too sensitive,"* whenever you raise a concern. Over time, this creates confusion and self-doubt, leaving you increasingly reliant on their version of events. A classic example of gaslighting is a narcissistic partner accusing the non-narcissistic partner of being the narcissist! Repeated accusations like this can make you question your own behavior and even your identity, keeping you trapped in a cycle of self-doubt and dependence.

The ultimate goal of gaslighting is control. By distorting your sense of reality, the gaslighter shifts power in their favor, making it difficult for you to trust your instincts or make independent decisions. The effects can be long-lasting, leaving emotional scars that make it hard to rebuild your confidence even after the relationship ends. Recognizing gaslighting early on is crucial; if you feel consistently confused, unheard, or blamed for things you didn't do, it's time to reevaluate the relationship and seek support.

11. Projection

Projection is another toxic behavior that shifts responsibility and blame away from the perpetrator, often leaving you questioning your own actions or feelings. Unlike gaslighting, which distorts your reality, projection involves attributing the toxic partner's traits, emotions, or actions to you. For example, a partner who feels insecure about their behavior might accuse you of being insecure, or someone who struggles with honesty might frequently accuse you of lying. This tactic keeps you focused on disproving their accusations rather than addressing their behavior.

The psychology behind projection often stems from the toxic partner's inability to confront their own flaws or feelings. By projecting these onto you, they avoid accountability while creating a narrative where you're at fault. The impact on you can be profound. Over time, you might internalize their accusations, questioning your own integrity or emotional stability. Recognizing projection allows you to step back and see the behavior for what it is: a deflection of responsibility. Instead of engaging in endless defense, shift your focus to identifying patterns and prioritizing your emotional well-being.

12. Emotional Manipulation

Emotional manipulation weaves guilt and obligation into the fabric of the relationship, making it difficult to set healthy boundaries. Your partner might play the victim, exaggerate their struggles to elicit sympathy, or imply that your love is proven only by prioritizing their needs. Statements like, *"If you really loved me, you'd do this,"* shift the emotional burden onto you, making you feel guilty for prioritizing your own well-being. They might share traumatic stories during conflicts to divert attention from their harmful behavior, ensuring the focus always stays on their pain rather than their actions.

In some cases, emotional manipulation can escalate into alarming territory, including threats of self-harm, actual self-harm such as cutting, or even threats of suicide. These actions are designed to heighten your sense of obligation and fear, trapping you in a cycle of guilt and responsibility for their emotional state. Such tactics create an environment where you feel you can never leave or set boundaries without dire consequences.

If you experience threats or acts of self-harm in your relationship, it is vital to seek support and tell someone you trust. Speak to a friend, family member, or professional counselor about what you're experiencing. You are not responsible for your partner's actions, and staying silent only reinforces the unhealthy dynamic. Protecting your mental and emotional health is essential, and reaching out for help is a crucial step toward breaking the cycle of manipulation.

13. Inconsistent Communication

Inconsistent communication introduces instability into the relationship, leaving you unsure where you stand. One week, your partner might shower you with attention and affection, texting constantly and planning romantic dates. The next, they become distant or unresponsive, offering no explanation for the shift. This hot-and-cold behavior creates an emotional rollercoaster as you work harder to regain their attention. For example, they might disappear for days without contact, only to return with affectionate messages as though nothing happened. Healthy relationships thrive on consistency and mutual effort; when communication feels unpredictable, it often signals deeper emotional unavailability or a need for control. Over time, this inconsistency keeps you emotionally off balance, making it harder to evaluate the relationship objectively.

14. Fear of Abandonment and Testing Boundaries

Some partners display a pattern of behaviors driven by an intense fear of abandonment, which can alternately pull you closer and push you away. This behavior often manifests as creating conflicts, canceling plans abruptly, or demanding constant reassurance of your commitment. For example, they might accuse you of neglecting them if you prioritize time with friends or family, framing your independence as a lack of care. These actions can leave you in a perpetual state of emotional vigilance, constantly striving to prove your devotion and avoid upsetting them.

The cycle is emotionally exhausting. It alternates between moments of intense affection, where they shower you with love and praise, and moments where they push boundaries or create conflict to test how far they can go before you'll leave. They might challenge your patience by making unreasonable demands, criticizing your actions, or even fabricating situations that require you to "prove" your loyalty. Over time, this dynamic erodes your emotional resilience, leaving you drained and questioning your sense of self.

Recognizing this pattern early is essential for evaluating whether the relationship is fostering personal growth or simply trapping you in a cycle of self-doubt and exhaustion. While the affection and praise may feel validating, it's important to ask whether these moments are genuine or part of a larger cycle designed to maintain control and keep you tethered to the relationship.

Although we are not trying to diagnose personality disorders, this behavior is a hallmark of Borderline Personality Disorder (BPD, see Chapter 5). Relationships with individuals exhibiting these patterns can be particularly challenging, as the emotional highs and lows are deeply tied to their unresolved fears. BPD is an incredibly difficult condition to navigate in relationships, often requiring professional support for both parties. If you recognize these behaviors, it's critical to consider whether the relationship aligns with your emotional health and well-being.

15. Splitting

Splitting is one of the most destabilizing behaviors in a toxic relationship, as it fractures your sense of connection and emotional safety.

In this dynamic, the toxic partner alternates between viewing you as their savior one moment and a villain the next, creating an emotional rollercoaster. For instance, they might praise you for being *"the only person who understands them"* one day, only to accuse you of betrayal over a minor disagreement the next.

Imagine planning a thoughtful surprise for your partner, only to be met with accusations of trying to outshine them. Alternatively, they might react with disproportionate anger to an innocuous comment, like forgetting a small detail about their day.

This pattern is particularly prevalent in individuals with borderline tendencies, where emotions run to extremes. It is perfectly possible to have a wonderful day out with your partner and drive them home, only for their mood to switch inexplicably to rage when you get there. No matter how much you attempt to calm them, it will be to no avail, and you'll find yourself leaving the scene with expletives ringing in your ears.

Splitting leaves you walking on eggshells, constantly trying to win back the version of your partner who adored you. Over time, this dynamic erodes your confidence as you internalize their shifting perceptions and blame yourself for their sudden changes in attitude. Recognizing this behavior is crucial, as it's a clear indicator of emotional instability and a lack of healthy conflict resolution skills.

16. Belittling or Invalidating Concerns

Belittling and invalidating your concerns often emerge subtly but leave a lasting impact. When the relationship has been ongoing for some weeks or a few months, your partner might start dismissing your emotions with statements like, *"You're overreacting,"* or *"Why do you always make everything about you?"* This tactic minimizes your feelings and shifts the focus away from their behavior, leaving you questioning your right to express your needs.

For instance, you might share frustration about their inconsistent communication, only for them to respond with, *"Well, maybe you're just too clingy,"* or *"You're being dramatic again."* Over time, this invalidation chips away at your confidence, making you hesitant to voice your concerns. The result is a growing sense of isolation and powerlessness, as your emotions are consistently dismissed as unimportant or excessive. A healthy partner acknowledges your feelings and works to address them; a toxic partner uses invalidation as a tool to silence you.

17. Excessive Criticism

Criticism in a toxic relationship often starts subtly, disguised as helpful suggestions or observations. However, as the relationship progresses, it becomes more pointed and relentless. Your partner might start by making comments like, *"You could dress a little better,"* or *"Why don't you ever try harder at work?"* These remarks evolve into harsher judgments about your personality, appearance, or choices, leaving you feeling inadequate. For example, they might ridicule your hobbies, dismiss your career ambitions, or criticize how you interact with others while claiming they're *"just being honest."*

This constant stream of criticism keeps you emotionally dependent as you find yourself striving to earn their approval and avoid their disapproval. It creates a dynamic where your self-worth is tied to their shifting standards, making it harder to see the relationship for what it truly is. While constructive feedback has a place in healthy relationships, excessive criticism is a tool for control, eroding your confidence and making you easier to manipulate.

18. Passive-Aggressiveness

Passive-aggressiveness is a covert way of asserting control and expressing dissatisfaction without directly addressing the issue. This behavior often leaves you feeling confused and unsure about where you stand. For instance, instead of saying they're upset about you canceling plans, your partner might say, *"It's fine; I didn't expect you to prioritize me anyway."* Or they may agree to do something grudgingly, only to sabotage it later, claiming, *"I was just trying to help, but it's obviously not good enough."*

Over time, this indirect communication creates a sense of unease as you try to decode their true feelings while avoiding further conflict. The lack of directness makes it nearly impossible to resolve issues, keeping you in a constant state of uncertainty. Passive-aggressiveness erodes trust and fosters resentment, as it denies you the opportunity for open, honest communication. In a healthy relationship, conflicts are addressed directly, not through veiled jabs or subtle digs.

19. Stonewalling

Stonewalling, or the refusal to engage in meaningful communication, is a particularly damaging behavior that shuts down the possibility of resolution. When your partner stonewalls, they might ignore your attempts to discuss an issue, walk out of the room mid-conversation, or give you the silent treatment for days on end. For example, they may refuse to answer your calls or texts after a disagreement, leaving you in emotional limbo.

This tactic leaves you feeling powerless, as every effort to address concerns is met with a wall of silence. It creates an environment where your feelings are dismissed and your voice is silenced, undermining any sense of partnership and over time, stonewalling fosters resentment and isolation, as it becomes clear that your emotional needs are not a priority. Healthy relationships require mutual engagement, even during conflict; stonewalling denies this, making it a red flag that should not be ignored.

20. Excessive Jealousy and Control

Excessive jealousy is often disguised as concern or protectiveness but can quickly escalate into possessiveness and control. For example, a partner might initially express mild discomfort about you spending time with a particular friend. Over time, this discomfort may evolve into accusations of disloyalty, demands to cut ties with long-standing friendships, or constant questioning about your whereabouts. They might frame their jealousy as a sign of love, saying things like, *"I just care about you too much to lose you,"* but the underlying intent is often about exerting control rather than expressing affection.

This behavior doesn't just target your social life; it can extend to your work, hobbies, and even family relationships. A partner consumed by jealousy may insist on monitoring your text messages, emails, or social media accounts, claiming it's necessary to build trust. Over time, their possessiveness can isolate you, leaving you dependent on them for emotional support. This dynamic erodes your autonomy and creates an environment of fear and submission. Healthy relationships thrive on mutual trust, not control. Let's be clear: it is never OK for someone to come into your life and tell you to cut ties with long-standing friends.

21. Inappropriate Levels of Rage

Rage that far outweighs the situation is a glaring red flag. Imagine forgetting to respond to a text, only to be met with an explosive outburst accusing you of neglect or disrespect. Inappropriate rage often emerges as a tool for intimidation, forcing you to tread carefully around your partner to avoid triggering their anger. For instance, they might throw objects, slam doors, or yell during minor disagreements, creating an atmosphere of fear.

This behavior doesn't just strain the relationship; it can have long-term emotional effects, leaving you anxious and hyper-vigilant. Over time, you might start to internalize their reactions, blaming yourself for their outbursts and adjusting your behavior to keep the peace.

However, no one deserves to live in a state of constant emotional tension. Recognizing these patterns early can help you set firm boundaries and prioritize your safety.

If your partner's rage ever escalates to physical violence, then you must tell someone and seek help.

22. False Accusations of Infidelity

Unfounded accusations of cheating or disloyalty can quickly destabilize a relationship. A partner who frequently accuses you of infidelity might be projecting their own insecurities or even their own unfaithful actions onto you. For instance, they might demand to know why you came home late, implying that your delay was due to an affair, even when you were simply stuck in traffic. These accusations create an environment of constant defensiveness, where you feel compelled to prove your loyalty repeatedly.

This dynamic often shifts the power balance in their favor, as their accusations force you to focus on reassuring them rather than addressing their behavior. In some cases, the allegations may serve as a diversion, drawing attention away from their own questionable actions. Over time, this tactic can erode your confidence, leaving you emotionally exhausted and questioning your own integrity. A partner who consistently projects mistrust is unlikely to foster the foundation of mutual respect and security that a healthy relationship requires.

23. Financial Manipulation

Financial manipulation often begins subtly, making it difficult to recognize at first. A partner might insist on managing shared finances, citing their expertise, or guilt you into covering expenses under the guise of financial hardship. For instance, they might claim, *"I've had such a tough month; can you handle rent again?"* While occasional financial support is normal in relationships, consistent patterns of dependency or control over money signal a deeper issue.

This behavior can escalate to restricting your access to funds, monitoring your spending, or even using finances as a tool to keep you from leaving. For example, they might discourage you from pursuing career opportunities, framing it as unnecessary because *"we'll always have each other."* Financial manipulation creates a dependency that makes it harder to leave, as you may feel trapped by limited resources or guilt. Healthy partnerships encourage financial transparency and mutual respect for independence.

24. Indifference to Your Achievements

A partner who shows little interest in or outright dismisses your successes can make you feel invisible or undervalued. For example, you might share news about a promotion at work, only for them to respond with a shrug or redirect the conversation back to themselves. This lack of enthusiasm for your accomplishments can create a sense of isolation, as though your milestones are insignificant or unworthy of celebration.

Over time, this indifference chips away at your confidence and joy, leaving you questioning your value in the relationship. A supportive partner celebrates your achievements and takes pride in your growth, fostering an environment of mutual encouragement and respect. Recognizing indifference early on lets you evaluate whether the relationship aligns with your emotional needs and aspirations.

25. Hypocrisy

Hypocrisy and double standards are hallmarks of toxic relationships, creating an unfair and destabilizing dynamic that undermines trust and emotional security. These behaviors occur when one partner imposes strict rules or expectations on the other while exempting themselves from the same standards. It's not just unfair; it's a deliberate form of control that leaves you questioning your judgment, feeling insecure, and constantly on edge.

A clear example is when a toxic partner demands that you cut ties with long-standing, reasonable friendships, particularly those involving ex-partners, even if those relationships have evolved into harmless and platonic connections. They may insist that these friendships are inappropriate or disloyal, accusing you of not prioritizing the relationship. At the same time, they might keep their own ex in their life, justifying it as *"different"* or *"necessary"* while maintaining secrecy around the nature of that connection. Worse still, they may claim they never contact their ex when in a relationship, a reassurance designed to keep you off guard, only to reengage with that ex, potentially for sex, when your relationship faces challenges.

This blatant hypocrisy erodes trust and emotional well-being, leaving you feeling isolated and anxious. Healthy relationships are built on mutual respect and consistent boundaries, where both partners are accountable to the same standards. There should be no one in your life, or theirs, that cannot be met in a relaxed and transparent way. When double standards emerge, they signal a lack of respect and fairness, which no relationship can thrive without.

26. Ghosting

Ghosting is one of the most hurtful behaviors in modern dating, especially when a relationship has been going well for a few weeks or months. It happens when someone suddenly cuts off all communication without explanation, leaving you in silence with no warning and no closure. This abrupt disappearance can be deeply painful, creating confusion and self-doubt. The sudden withdrawal of contact is particularly difficult because it offers no resolution, making it easy to become stuck in a cycle of overanalyzing what went wrong. Many people find themselves replaying conversations, searching for clues, and wondering if they did something to cause it. The lack of closure can make it incredibly hard to move on. However, it is important to remember that ghosting is rarely about you. It usually reflects the other person's inability or unwillingness to communicate honestly or handle emotional discomfort in a mature way.

Dealing with the lack of closure is challenging, but it can help to reframe the situation. Instead of seeing ghosting as a reflection of your worth, consider it a sign that this person was never capable of a healthy relationship. In many ways, their silence provides the answer you need. Rather than chasing an explanation or waiting for them to return, it is healthier to accept that they have removed themselves from your life for a reason. If they were unable to offer the basic respect of a direct conversation, they were never the right person for you. While it may not feel like it in the moment, ghosting can sometimes be a blessing in disguise. It spares you from investing further in someone who was never truly present, allowing you to move forward and seek relationships where communication and respect are a priority.

When Do Problematic Behaviors Add Up to Abuse?

Toxic relationships aren't defined by a single issue but by repeated patterns of harmful behaviors that create a profoundly unbalanced dynamic. The more of these behaviors you experience, such as hypocrisy, double standards, gaslighting, splitting, rage, emotional manipulation, coercive control, and so on, the more the relationship begins to shift from unhealthy to outright abusive.

When faced with these repeated patterns, it's crucial to reevaluate the relationship seriously as it is unlikely to improve and is, in fact, likely to worsen over time. No amount of effort on your part can fix a partner who lacks insight or refuses to change. Healthy relationships are built on fairness, trust, mutual respect, and accountability. If those qualities are consistently missing and replaced by manipulation, control, and harm, it's a clear signal that the relationship is toxic and cannot offer the safety or security you deserve.

4

Red Flag Behaviors on Social Media

You must also tune your **red flag radar** to social media interactions. Social media has become a significant extension of modern relationships, but it can also be a powerful platform for manipulation, projection, and control. While technology can enhance connection, it can also amplify insecurities, unhealthy dynamics, and toxic behaviors. It's important to recognize when social media use shifts from fostering a connection to being a tool for control or emotional harm. Seven common red flag behaviors to watch for are:

1. Monitoring and Surveillance

Partners with controlling tendencies may use social media to monitor your activities excessively. This goes beyond casual curiosity, manifesting as constant scrutiny of your posts, comments, likes, and interactions. They may question why you liked a specific post or demand explanations for casual comments, framing it as a concern for your well-being. Over time, this can create a sense of surveillance and mistrust, eroding your autonomy and making you feel as though you are under constant watch.

2. Trawling Through Your History

Being curious about a new partner's social media activity is natural, but some individuals take this too far. Trawling involves going back years or even decades through your posts, not out of genuine interest but to find inconsistencies or supposed "evidence" of dishonesty. For example, they might accuse you of lying about a past relationship based on an old photo or a comment taken out of context. This behavior often indicates a lack of trust and a need for control, turning social media into a weapon for creating conflict rather than fostering understanding.

3. Public Criticism and Shaming

A partner who uses social media to air grievances or criticize you publicly demonstrates a lack of respect for your privacy and dignity. This could involve posting passive-aggressive memes, vague statuses that clearly reference your behavior, or even direct attacks designed to embarrass or humiliate you in front of others. These actions can harm your self-esteem and create feelings of isolation, as they involve your personal issues being put on display for others to see.

4. Triangulation Through Online Engagement

Some partners use social media to introduce feelings of jealousy or inadequacy, a tactic known as triangulation. This might involve excessively liking, commenting on, or interacting with others' posts in flirtatious or inappropriate ways while ignoring or minimizing their interactions with you. Such behavior is designed to make you feel insecure and question your worth in the relationship, further consolidating their control over your emotions.

5. Projection of their Issues

Toxic individuals often use social media to project their own flaws onto others. For instance, a narcissistic partner might frequently share posts about *'10 ways to spot narcissists'* or *'how to avoid toxic people on online dating sites'* while simultaneously engaging in those exact behaviors. Apart from the irony leaving you incredulous, this creates confusion and cognitive dissonance, making you question your own perceptions of their actions. It's a subtle but effective way to deflect accountability while sowing doubt in your ability to trust your instincts.

6. Love Bombing and Its Social Media Shadow

As noted in previous chapters, in the early stages of a relationship, some partners may engage in love bombing, overwhelming you with attention and affection, both in private and on social media. While this can initially feel flattering, it often shifts abruptly to withholding or public devaluation once they've established control. Be wary of partners who use social media as a stage for exaggerated displays of affection that seem performative rather than genuine, as these behaviors often serve a manipulative purpose.

7. Subtle Isolation Through Social Media

Some partners may subtly or overtly pressure you to limit your social media activity, framing it as a way to protect your relationship or maintain privacy. They might discourage you from posting selfies, interacting with friends, or sharing aspects of your life that don't directly involve them. Over time, this behavior can isolate you from your support network, giving them greater control over your life and diminishing your sense of independence.

Recognizing Healthy Social Media Dynamics

Social media should be a space where you feel supported, respected, and free to express yourself. Healthy dynamics involve mutual trust, open communication, and boundaries that protect each partner's autonomy. If your partner's online behavior consistently causes you to feel doubt, anxiety, or unease, it's a clear sign to address the issue directly or reassess the relationship entirely.

5

Personality Disorders and Associated Behaviors

Where might these problematic behaviors originate? Previous chapters explored the toxic relationship cycle and the offline and online behaviors that can emerge within it. In some cases, the root of these patterns may be a personality disorder, and these will be introduced in this chapter. These conditions shape how a person thinks, feels, and interacts with others in ways that are often rigid, intense, challenging, and difficult to change.

While not everyone who exhibits concerning behaviors has a diagnosable disorder, understanding that personality disorders exist can provide valuable insight. Some individuals may display traits such as manipulation, impulsivity, or emotional volatility without meeting the threshold for a formal diagnosis, while others may qualify due to the severity and consistency of their behavior. In practical terms, the distinction matters less than the impact these behaviors have on you. Whether someone is difficult, dysfunctional, or clinically diagnosable, the result can still be confusion, distress, and harm.

This chapter is not about diagnosing anyone but is included for awareness, insight, and context. Recognizing these patterns can help you gain clarity, step out of self-doubt, and understand when a dynamic is driven by the other person's psychological makeup rather than anything you have done. Awareness allows you to set boundaries, make informed choices, and protect your well-being.

A person with a personality disorder has long-standing unhealthy patterns of thought, emotion, and behavior that often disrupt relationships and create significant challenges in building successful romantic connections. According to the *Diagnostic and Statistical Manual of Mental Disorders* (Fifth Edition, DSM-5, American Psychiatric Association, 2013), personality disorders are categorized into three clusters:

Cluster A: The Eccentric and Detached

Cluster A personality disorders include Paranoid, Schizoid, and Schizotypal Personality Disorders. Individuals with traits from this Cluster often appear eccentric or socially detached, and their behavior may be interpreted as odd or aloof. Although these disorders share some similarities with schizophrenia, they are distinct in that they do not typically involve the severe psychosis or disconnection from reality that defines schizophrenia. Instead, Cluster A traits are more about enduring patterns of suspicion, isolation, or unusual thinking that, while disruptive to relationships, do not reach the level of a full-blown psychotic disorder.

Common Behaviors Associated with Cluster A:

- **Paranoid Personality Disorder:** Marked by a pervasive distrust and suspicion of others. Individuals may misinterpret harmless comments or actions as malicious or threatening. For example, they might question your intentions over minor misunderstandings or insist that you're hiding something from them, even in the absence of evidence. This constant suspicion can make it very difficult

to build trust, and a stable relationship with someone with this disorder is unlikely.
- **Schizoid Personality Disorder:** Characterized by a preference for solitude and a lack of interest in close relationships. Someone with schizoid traits may seem emotionally distant or indifferent, avoiding emotional intimacy and preferring solitary activities over shared experiences. For instance, they might avoid social outings or express little interest in deepening social connections. Because they prefer solitude, you are very unlikely to cross paths with someone with this disorder on an online dating site.
- **Schizotypal Personality Disorder:** Involving odd beliefs, eccentric behaviour, and difficulties with interpersonal connections. This could manifest as peculiar ways of speaking, unusual hobbies or interests, or a belief in magical thinking: for example, attributing special meaning to coincidences or believing they can read minds. These traits can make interactions feel unpredictable or unsettling.

Cluster A Traits in Online Dating:

When it comes to dating platforms, individuals with Cluster A traits are less likely to engage actively. Their preference for solitude and discomfort with social interaction means they will likely be underrepresented in the fast-paced, socially demanding world of online dating. However, you might encounter someone with these traits in niche or interest-focused communities, particularly those centered around shared hobbies or intellectual pursuits.

While their behaviors may not always be harmful, they can make forming a close and connected relationship challenging. You might find that their emotional unavailability, reluctance to engage in social settings, or lack of reciprocity leaves you feeling isolated or undervalued. For example:

PERSONALITY DISORDERS AND ASSOCIATED BEHAVIORS

- Someone with **paranoid tendencies** might question your motives for joining the platform or repeatedly seek reassurance that you're not misleading them. They are very likely to accuse you of infidelity without basis.
- An individual with **schizoid traits** might engage minimally in conversations, avoiding deeper discussions or shared experiences, which can lead to feelings of emotional stagnation.
- A person with **schizotypal behaviors** might express ideas or beliefs that seem confusing or unconventional, making it difficult to find common ground.

Being aware of these traits allows you to recognize when someone's behavior stems from a deeper pattern of detachment or eccentricity. While these traits may not always indicate harm, they can serve as an early indicator that the relationship may not meet your emotional or social needs.

Cluster B: The Dramatic and Erratic

Cluster B personality disorders include Narcissistic, Borderline, Histrionic, and Antisocial Personality Disorders. These individuals often exhibit dramatic, emotional, or erratic behaviors that can be intensely captivating at first but may lead to significant challenges in relationships over time. Cluster B traits are more likely to be encountered in online dating environments, as individuals with these characteristics often present themselves as charismatic, confident, or exciting.

Common Behaviors Associated with Cluster B:

- **Narcissistic Personality Disorder:** Marked by grandiosity, a need for admiration, and a lack of empathy. Someone with narcissistic traits might dominate conversations, focus heavily on their own achievements, or belittle your accomplishments. They may also use manipulation tactics, such as gaslighting, or accuse you of being narcissistic to deflect blame.

- **Borderline Personality Disorder:** Characterized by emotional instability, fear of abandonment, and impulsive behaviors. For example, a partner with borderline traits may idealize you one moment and devalue you the next, creating a rollercoaster of emotions. These emotions can be intense and fast-changing; within minutes, they can go from sweet and loving to downright rageful. Fear of abandonment may lead to clinginess, excessive reassurance-seeking, or testing boundaries.
- **Histrionic Personality Disorder:** Involving excessive attention-seeking and overly dramatic behavior. A partner with histrionic traits might make everything about them, demand constant validation, or escalate minor issues into significant dramas to gain attention.
- **Antisocial Personality Disorder:** Defined by a disregard for the rights of others and manipulative tendencies. It's important to distinguish between Antisocial Personality Disorder and psychopathy. While both involve manipulative and often harmful behaviors, psychopathy typically includes a lack of remorse and a more calculated approach to deception. Though rare, individuals with these traits can be dangerous, using charm to mask their true intentions and engaging in exploitative or harmful actions without concern for the consequences.

Cluster B Traits in Online Dating:

Individuals with Cluster B traits are more likely to actively engage on dating platforms, often crafting highly appealing profiles that showcase their charm and confidence. However, their behaviors may include:

- **Excessive Charm:** Overwhelming attention or grand gestures early in the relationship that feel too good to be true.
- **Emotional Volatility:** Unpredictable mood swings, from extreme affection to sudden anger or withdrawal.
- **Manipulative Tactics:** Using guilt, fear, or flattery to gain control or influence your decisions.

A relationship with someone who is Cluster B will very likely follow the trajectory of the toxic relationship cycle in one way or another. Many problematic behaviors, both online and offline, will manifest themselves and be highly destabilizing. Further complicating matters, these individuals have very little insight into their condition and their impact on you. Even if they do recognize something is not quite right, they are unlikely to be motivated to do anything about it. This is important because it means that their behavior will not improve for the better.

Cluster C: The Anxious and Fearful

Cluster C personality disorders include Avoidant, Dependent, and Obsessive-Compulsive Personality Disorders. Individuals with traits from this Cluster often exhibit behaviors rooted in anxiety, fear, and a need for control or reassurance. While these traits may not always seem harmful, they can create emotional strain and imbalance in a relationship over time.

Common Behaviors Associated with Cluster C:

- **Avoidant Personality Disorder:** Marked by extreme sensitivity to rejection and avoidance of social interactions. Someone with avoidant traits might struggle to open up emotionally or avoid conflict altogether, leaving issues unresolved.

- **Dependent Personality Disorder:** Characterized by an excessive need to be taken care of and difficulty making independent decisions. A partner with dependent traits may rely on you for constant reassurance or avoid making choices without your input, creating an imbalanced dynamic.
- **Obsessive-Compulsive Personality Disorder:** Defined by perfectionism, rigidity, and a need for control. For example, they might insist on doing things their way, dismissing your preferences or needs, and becoming upset when routines are disrupted.

Cluster C Traits in Online Dating:

Individuals with Cluster C traits may approach relationships cautiously and could be underrepresented on dating platforms. Their behaviors might include:

- **Excessive Caution:** It takes a long time to progress in the relationship due to fear of rejection.
- **Over-Reliance:** Seeking constant reassurance or validation to feel secure in the relationship.
- **Rigidity:** Insistence of strict routines or preferences that leave little room for compromise.

While these traits may not be as immediately harmful as others, they can still create challenges in forming a balanced, healthy relationship.

Origins of Personality Disorders

Personality disorders often stem from early life experiences, such as childhood trauma, abuse, neglect, or unstable relationships with caregivers. These experiences can shape how individuals view themselves, others, and the world, leading to the enduring patterns of behavior that define these disorders.

If someone you're dating shares that they've experienced significant early-life trauma, it's natural and kind to approach this with empathy and understanding. However, it's equally important to stay alert for troubling behaviors. While not everyone with a difficult past exhibits problematic traits, these early experiences can contribute to the development of the patterns and disorders outlined in this chapter.

It's also worth emphasizing that personality disorders are serious mental health conditions that, in some cases, can cause profound suffering for those who experience them. While compassion is crucial, your role is not to absorb mistreatment or accept harmful behavior because of someone else's struggles. Protecting your emotional well-being should remain a priority.

Behavior Over Diagnosis

Recall that the goal here is not to help you diagnose your prospective or new partner or anyone else with a personality disorder. Diagnosing a personality disorder is a complex process that requires extensive professional expertise and a thorough understanding of an individual's history and the context of their behavior. It's also worth noting that personality disorders exist on a spectrum, can overlap, and involve patterns that have typically been present since adolescence or early adulthood. All of this adds significant complication to the brief overview presented in this book, and it won't surprise you to know that very few individuals fit neatly into any one personality disorder.

In any case, for us, the diagnosis itself is irrelevant. What matters most is the behavior you are experiencing or watching out for and how it impacts your emotional well-being. This book emphasizes awareness of problematic behaviors, many of which may arise from traits associated with personality disorders. So, while it's helpful to understand that these disorders exist and may inform specific patterns of behavior, your focus should remain on recognizing and responding to the behaviors rather than attempting to label or diagnose them.

If you do suspect that your new partner or date may have a personality disorder, it's essential to understand a few key points:

- **You can't diagnose them.** Even if certain traits or behaviors align with what you've read or learned, diagnosing a personality disorder requires professional evaluation. More importantly, such a label will not change the reality of what you are experiencing in the relationship.
- **You won't be able to fix or change them.** Many individuals with personality disorders lack the insight and self-awareness to recognize their behaviors or understand their impact on others. Any attempts to raise these concerns are unlikely to be welcomed and may provoke defensiveness or hostility. They may even turn the blame on you, accusing you of being the problem.
- **It's not your role to help or save them.** Even if someone acknowledges their struggles, meaningful change requires professional intervention and a genuine desire on their part to seek help. Your role in a relationship is not to endure mistreatment or take on the burden of someone else's emotional challenges.

Prevalence of Personality Disorders on Dating Platforms

It is impossible to know for sure the prevalence of personality-disordered individuals on a dating platform. That said, your chances of running into these people might be higher than you realize. Let's make some educated guesses.

It is reasonable to estimate that Cluster B personality disorders affect around 5% of the general population. This statistic suggests that if you swipe through 100 profiles, you may encounter five individuals exhibiting traits consistent with these conditions. Moreover, your chances of attempting to match with these individuals are probably a bit higher because their charismatic or attention-grabbing profiles may increase the likelihood of getting your attention. Awareness of this possibility is not about fostering fear but encouraging mindfulness as you navigate the dating world.

6

Making Sense of the Toxic Relationship Cycle and Behaviors

If you're reading this, you might be at a crossroads and questioning a current or recent relationship or trying to make sense of something that feels inexplicably wrong. For those new to online dating, the descriptions of toxic relationship cycles and behaviors can feel shocking, even surreal. You might wonder, *"How could someone try so hard in a relationship, be so accommodating, giving, and invested, only to be disrespected so profoundly?"* The idea that someone could intentionally engage in behaviors like love bombing, gaslighting, or triangulation might feel impossible to comprehend. Surely, no one could *deliberately* act this way, right?

It's natural to ask yourself: *"How does this even happen?"* *"How could anyone get stuck in such a relationship?"* Maybe you're thinking, *"It would never happen to me. I'd see the signs. I'd rationalize and leave."* Yet, if you've found yourself in such a situation, you might be asking, *"Why am I still here?"* or *"How is this happening to me?"* These are difficult, painful questions, and it's tempting to blame yourself for not recognizing the red flags earlier or for not walking away sooner.

But here's the truth: toxic relationships are not as simple as they seem from the outside. The toxic relationship cycle—idealization, devaluation, and discard—is designed to confuse, destabilize, and trap you in a web of emotional dependency. It's not a reflection of your intelligence, strength, or worth. Instead, it reflects how these behaviors are crafted to bypass your rational mind and tap into your emotional vulnerabilities. It's why the cycle is so powerful and why so many smart, loving, and capable people find themselves stuck.

In the following sections, we'll explore the answers to these questions. You'll gain insight into how toxic behaviors manifest, why they feel so disorienting, and why leaving isn't as simple as it might seem. We'll also address whether these behaviors are intentional or instinctive and how someone could flip so drastically from being a loving partner to someone who devalues and discards you. Most importantly, you'll discover why self-blame is not the answer.

Remember to be gentle with yourself if you recognize yourself in any of this. Blaming yourself for being in this situation is not only unhelpful, it's unfair. You didn't choose to be manipulated or mistreated. The fact that you're here, seeking understanding, means you're taking the first steps toward clarity, healing, and reclaiming your sense of self.

This chapter isn't about judgment; it's about making sense of something profoundly confusing and painful. Together, we'll unpack these dynamics so you can begin to understand what happened, why it happened, and how to move forward with compassion for yourself.

Toxic Behavior: Conscious or Unconscious?

Reading about toxic relationships can feel like stepping into a parallel world you never imagined or could never imagine being part of. If you're beginning to realize you're in such a relationship (or reflecting on a recent one), it's natural to wonder: *"Were they consciously manipulative, or was this behavior a product of their own pain and unresolved issues?"* or *"Could someone honestly act this way intentionally?"* The truth is, you may never know for sure, and focusing too much on their intent can distract you from what's truly important: the effect their actions have had on you.

When caught in a toxic dynamic, analyzing and rationalizing their behavior is tempting. You might think, *"Maybe they didn't mean it. Maybe they're just struggling. Perhaps if I understand them better, I can help them change".* But this thinking keeps you focused on them, not yourself. It keeps you tied to the relationship, searching for reasons instead of recognizing the patterns of harm. What matters most isn't whether their actions were conscious or unconscious; it's the impact on your sense of self, boundaries, and emotional well-being. The patterns of toxic relationships, intentional or not, damage your confidence and undermine your ability to trust your own instincts.

You can find yourself caught in an emotional whirlwind, constantly trying to regain the love and connection you experienced initially. This is where trauma bonding takes hold. The alternating highs and lows of affection and rejection create a powerful attachment that feels impossible to break. Understanding how trauma bonds form and why they feel so overwhelming is essential for breaking free from these cycles and reclaiming your sense of self.

The Danger of Trauma Bonding

One of the most insidious aspects of toxic relationships is trauma bonding. This deeply entrenched emotional attachment forms through alternating cycles of affection and rejection, creating a connection that is as powerful as it is damaging. Trauma bonding doesn't just exploit your emotions; it hijacks your brain's chemical responses and thought patterns, leaving you trapped in a cycle from which it is hard to escape. And no matter how strong, rational, or well-balanced you believe yourself to be, it's important not to underestimate the power of a trauma bond: it can entrap anyone!

At the heart of trauma bonding is intermittent reinforcement, where affection and rejection are alternated unpredictably. This inconsistency mirrors addiction, triggering the release of dopamine, the brain's reward chemical, during moments of love or reconciliation. These highs are intoxicating, often overshadowing the lows of criticism, rejection, and manipulation. Like a gambler chasing the next jackpot, you find yourself clinging to the hope that the next high, the return of affection or the idealized version of your partner, will make the pain worthwhile.

Oxytocin, the bonding hormone, further strengthens this attachment. Released during moments of intimacy, physical affection, or comfort, it deepens your trust and attachment to the toxic partner, even as they cause harm. Meanwhile, the constant unpredictability and tension elevate levels of cortisol, the stress hormone. This keeps your body in a heightened state of alertness, leaving you emotionally and physically dependent on the very person who is causing your distress.

Adding to this complexity is the role of cognitive dissonance. This psychological phenomenon occurs when your beliefs or values conflict with your reality, creating mental discomfort. For example, you may believe, *"They love me, they said so. They showed it initially!"* Yet their current behavior suggests the opposite. To resolve this conflict, your mind often downplays or rationalizes the toxic behavior, convincing you that things will improve or that the good times outweigh the bad. This internal struggle further entraps you, making it harder to see the situation clearly or take decisive action.

Hope for change also fuels trauma bonding. You may find yourself believing that if you just try harder, give more, or adjust your behavior, the relationship will return to its idealized phase. This belief is reinforced by the toxic partner's occasional displays of affection, remorse, or kindness, breadcrumbs designed to keep you emotionally invested. These gestures feel like progress but are part of the cycle, not genuine efforts to change.

Another key factor is the erosion of self-worth. Constant criticism, blame-shifting, and manipulation leave you questioning your value. Over time, you may internalize their negative messages, convincing yourself that you're undeserving of better or that the relationship's dysfunction is somehow your fault. This diminished sense of self makes it harder to imagine life outside the relationship or believe you have the strength to leave.

Fear of loneliness compounds this struggle. By the time the relationship reaches its most damaging stages, the toxic partner has often isolated you from your support network. Whether subtly or overtly, they may have distanced you from friends and family or made you feel as though no one else understands you. Without a strong safety net, the idea of leaving might feel overwhelming.

Finally, shame can paralyze you. Even when you recognize the harm being done, you may feel embarrassed or guilty for staying. You might think, *"How could I let this happen? Why didn't I leave sooner?"* The thought of confiding in loved ones and hearing them urge you to leave can feel unbearable, especially if you don't feel ready. This shame further isolates you, tightening the trauma bond and making it even harder to break free.

Understanding that trauma bonding is not a reflection of weakness is crucial. It is a complex combination of emotional, psychological, and chemical forces that can entrap even the strongest and most rational individuals. The interplay of dopamine, oxytocin, cortisol, cognitive dissonance, and hope creates a bond that feels unbreakable. But with awareness and support, it is possible to break free. Recognizing the patterns and understanding the mechanisms at play is the first step toward regaining your sense of self, rebuilding your confidence, and moving toward a healthier future.

Should You Galvanize Yourself to Leave?

If you're in a toxic relationship that's still new, just a few weeks or months old, the answer to whether you should leave is an unequivocal *yes*. At this stage, it's far easier to walk away than it will be later. The ties are still loose, and you're not yet practically entangled in ways that make leaving complicated.

Toxic relationships thrive on deepening your dependency, whether emotionally, financially, or socially. If you stay, the bond will only grow stronger, and the behaviors you're seeing now are unlikely to improve. Acting now allows you to protect yourself before the relationship becomes something that feels impossible to escape.

Leaving is particularly urgent if you're starting to feel pressured to make commitments, such as moving in together, merging finances, or planning for the future. If you've noticed behaviors that make you uneasy, trust your instincts. Don't dismiss red flags or wait for things to "settle down." Overcommitting, whether by moving to a new area, buying property together, or, most significantly, having children, can entangle you in exponentially more complex ways to untangle later.

If you've already started rationalizing their behavior or ignoring your own discomfort, pause and reflect. Are you staying because of what the relationship *is* or because of what you *hope* it could become? The longer you wait, the more difficult it will be to leave as emotional bonds deepen and practical commitments grow.

For those who have been in toxic relationships for years, the decision to leave is far more complex. Shared responsibilities, children, or deeply intertwined lives mean walking away requires careful planning and significant support. If you're in that situation, your journey will look very different, and seeking help from professionals, such as therapists or legal advisors, is essential.

But if you're in the early stages of a toxic relationship, the advice is clear: *leave now*. It's far better to face the short-term discomfort of ending things than to stay and risk losing more of yourself over time.

The sooner you act, the easier it will be to reclaim your independence and rebuild your confidence.

How to Exit and Rebuild from a Toxic Relationship

Leaving a toxic relationship, even one that is relatively new, can feel daunting, but the sooner you take action, the easier it will be to break free. Acting decisively protects your emotional well-being and prevents further entanglement. The longer you remain in an unhealthy relationship, the more difficult it becomes to detach as emotional bonds deepen and the toxic cycle strengthens. Recognizing the signs, setting firm boundaries, and focusing on your independence will help you move forward with clarity and strength.

The first step in leaving is acknowledging the patterns that have made the relationship harmful. If you have experienced love bombing, gaslighting, boundary violations, or unpredictable shifts between affection and criticism, understand that these behaviors are unlikely to improve with time. Toxic relationships follow a predictable cycle, and hoping for change will only prolong your suffering. Accepting that these dynamics will not change helps you detach emotionally and commit to leaving for good.

Reaching out for support is crucial during this process. Toxic relationships often thrive in isolation, making it easier for your partner to manipulate and control you. Do not let fear of judgment or embarrassment keep you from confiding in a trusted friend, family member, or therapist. An outside perspective can offer clarity, validate your feelings, and remind you that you deserve better. The act of reconnecting with supportive people is a powerful step toward breaking free.

Once you have made the decision to leave, set clear and firm boundaries. This is where the "no contact" strategy becomes essential. No contact means cutting off all communication, including texts, calls, emails, and social media interactions. It may feel harsh or extreme, but it is the most effective way to protect yourself from being drawn back in. Toxic partners often try to reengage with apologies, promises of change, or emotional manipulation. Without contact, they lose the ability to influence you, allowing you to regain control of your life. If no contact is not entirely possible due to shared responsibilities, such as co-parenting, minimize communication to only what is necessary and keep interactions as neutral as possible.

Acting quickly is key to avoiding deeper emotional entanglement. If you have not yet made long-term commitments such as moving in together, combining finances, or planning a future, take action before these ties make leaving more complicated. The longer you stay, the harder it becomes to walk away without significant upheaval. Making the decision now is an act of self-preservation and ensures that you can move forward with greater ease.

Leaving a toxic relationship is not just about physical separation; it is about rebuilding your independence and sense of self. Rediscovering your identity is a crucial part of healing. Focus on activities that bring you joy and reconnect with passions that may have been neglected during the relationship. Spending time with friends, engaging in hobbies, and pursuing goals that make you feel strong and capable will help restore confidence. Each step toward reclaiming your independence reinforces that you are more than what the relationship made you believe.

Resisting reengagement is one of the greatest challenges after leaving. Toxic partners often attempt to pull you back in by reminding you of the "good times" or claiming they have changed. Nostalgia can cloud judgment, making it tempting to believe that things could be different. Stay committed to your decision and remind yourself why you left. Actual change requires consistent effort and accountability, not just words or temporary gestures. Returning will only restart the toxic cycle and set back your healing process.

Once you have separated yourself from a toxic relationship, the next stage is healing and rebuilding your confidence. Lingering doubts and insecurities can make it difficult to trust again, but working through past experiences allows you to approach future relationships with clarity rather than fear.

Healing begins with acknowledging and processing past pain. Suppressing emotions does not make them disappear; instead, it prolongs their impact. Give yourself permission to feel what you need to feel. Journaling, speaking with a therapist, or confiding in a trusted friend can help you gain perspective and recognize how the relationship affected you. Understanding your emotions rather than avoiding them is a necessary step toward moving forward.

Rebuilding self-worth is another critical part of the process. Toxic relationships can erode confidence, making you question your value and ability to make good decisions. Reconnecting with activities that bring you joy, setting personal goals, and surrounding yourself with supportive people will help you rebuild a strong sense of self. Every step you take toward prioritizing your well-being reinforces that you deserve respect, care, and love.

Recognizing patterns and triggers from past relationships prevents the same mistakes from repeating. If you have a history of being drawn to emotionally unavailable partners or tend to overcompensate in relationships, becoming aware of these tendencies allows you to make healthier choices. Things like fear of abandonment or excusing bad behavior in the hope of change can lead to emotional reactions that cloud judgment. Developing awareness around these patterns helps you respond thoughtfully rather than falling into familiar but harmful dynamics.

Taking your time before entering a new relationship is one of the most critical steps toward ensuring that you do not repeat past mistakes.

Rushing into something new to fill an emotional void often leads to the same unhealthy patterns resurfacing. Giving yourself space to heal allows you to approach dating with confidence and a clearer understanding of what you need in a partner. Moving forward with intention rather than desperation creates the opportunity for a healthier, more fulfilling relationship.

Exiting a toxic relationship is not just about leaving someone behind; it is about choosing yourself. It is about reclaiming your independence, healing from the past, and rebuilding your confidence so that your future relationships are rooted in respect and mutual care. When you invest in your own well-being, you set the stage for the kind of love and partnership that genuinely supports and uplifts you.

Moving forward

In the next chapter, we'll explore how to avoid getting into a toxic relationship in the first place. By learning to recognize red flags, set healthy boundaries, and build self-awareness, you can protect yourself and create connections that are grounded in respect, care, and mutual understanding.

7

Recognizing Patterns and Protecting Yourself

Pattern spotting
Spotting problematic behaviors isn't about being hypercritical; it's about identifying patterns that undermine your emotional health. Repeated behaviors are rarely accidental and should not be ignored. A helpful mantra to guide you is:

If a behavior happens once, it might be an unfortunate occurrence; if it happens twice, it could be an unfortunate coincidence; but if it happens three times, it's a pattern and, therefore, a problem.

Inconsistent communication can be a significant red flag. Let's say your new partner starts the relationship with constant attention, texts you throughout the day, and expresses their enthusiasm for seeing you. Then, seemingly out of nowhere, they pull back and become distant, leaving your messages unanswered for days. If this cycle of hot-and-cold behavior happens once, it could be attributed to a busy schedule. If it happens twice, you might wonder if they're genuinely interested. But if it becomes a recurring pattern, it signals emotional unavailability or a deeper issue with commitment.

Excessive jealousy is another behavior to watch out for. A single comment about your interactions with a friend might seem like insecurity or a passing concern. If it happens again, with accusations about your loyalty or probing questions about your social life, you may start to feel uneasy. By the third time, when they insist you cut ties with a long-standing friend or monitor your whereabouts, their jealousy has shifted into controlling behavior, and this pattern should not be ignored.

Recognizing patterns also applies to how someone handles conflict. If a partner consistently responds to disagreements with inappropriate levels of rage, belittles your concerns, or deflects blame onto you, these behaviors can form a toxic pattern. For example, a minor disagreement might escalate into an outburst where they yell or slam doors. The second time, they might mock your feelings or dismiss your attempts to communicate. By the third instance, you might find yourself walking on eggshells, afraid to address issues for fear of triggering another reaction. These patterns of conflict resolution, or lack thereof, can severely damage your emotional well-being over time.

The key to recognizing patterns is to look at the broader picture rather than isolated incidents. Everyone makes mistakes or behaves poorly at times. Still, consistent repetition of harmful behaviors clearly indicates that something deeper is at play. Whether it's gaslighting, inconsistent communication, excessive jealousy, or emotional manipulation, identifying these patterns allows you to make informed decisions about whether the relationship is healthy and sustainable.

Paying attention to repeated behaviors gives you the clarity needed to protect your emotional health. Remember, acknowledging a pattern doesn't mean you must act immediately, but you should evaluate the situation carefully and consider whether this is the kind of relationship you want to invest in. Awareness is your first and most powerful tool in navigating these dynamics.

Protecting Yourself

Protecting yourself requires proactive effort, whether you're exploring online dating or navigating a new relationship. Here are some strategies to safeguard your emotional well-being:

- **Trust Your Instincts:** If something feels off, don't dismiss it. Your intuition is a valuable tool for recognizing red flags. For example, if your gut tells you that a partner's sudden withdrawal after an intense beginning feels manipulative, listen to that inner voice—it often picks up on subtle cues your conscious mind may overlook.
- **Set Clear Boundaries:** Be upfront about your limits and expectations. Healthy relationships respect boundaries; problematic ones test or dismiss them. For instance, if you make it clear that you value your friendships and a partner tries to isolate you or criticize those relationships, it's a sign that your boundaries are not being respected.
- **Take Your Time:** Resist the urge to rush into intimacy or commitment. Allow patterns to emerge over time, providing a clearer picture of the person's character. A partner who pushes for immediate declarations of love or demands exclusivity within days may be attempting to fast-track emotional dependency.
- **Pay Attention to Actions:** Consistency between words and actions is a hallmark of emotional stability. Observe whether someone's behavior aligns with their promises. For example, if they say they value open communication but shut down or become defensive during difficult conversations, this inconsistency is worth noting.
- **Stay Connected to Your Support System:** Problematic partners often try to isolate you from friends and family, so maintaining those connections is vital. Talk to trusted loved ones about your

relationship—they can provide valuable perspective. They may notice red flags that you've overlooked.

Moving Forward

Navigating relationships, whether online or in person, requires more than just recognizing red flags—it demands the ability to set clear boundaries and foster connections that are healthy, respectful, and fulfilling. The next section focuses on these essential skills. Chapter 8 explores how to establish and maintain boundaries, protecting yourself from harmful dynamics while creating the conditions for trust and emotional safety. Boundaries are not about building walls; they are about ensuring that your needs and values are respected from the outset. Chapter 9 then shifts the focus to what makes a relationship genuinely healthy. Moving beyond the avoidance of toxic behaviors, it explores the foundations of trust, mutual support, and emotional security. Together, these chapters will help you approach dating and relationships with confidence and to cultivate meaningful connections.

II

Part Two

Dating Well

8

Setting Boundaries and Protecting Yourself

The excitement of a new relationship can be intoxicating. When you meet someone who is charismatic, attractive, and makes you feel special, it is easy to get swept up in the moment. The early stages of attraction can create a powerful illusion that this person is exactly what you have been looking for. Chemistry and passion can make you overlook warning signs, dismiss differences that seem small at first, and believe that love will bridge any gaps in values or lifestyle.

But reality does not work that way. If you later find that your partner holds fundamentally different beliefs, disrespects your personal boundaries, or does not value the things that are important to you, it is not their fault. It is yours for not recognizing those differences sooner. People rarely change their core values, and expecting someone to become a different person just because you are in a relationship with them is unrealistic. Heartbreak often comes not from who someone is but from who you assumed they could be.

Setting boundaries is about protecting yourself from that kind of disappointment. Boundaries are not about control or restriction. They are about ensuring that your needs, values, and well-being are respected within a relationship. When you have clear boundaries, you are less likely to waste time on incompatible relationships, and more likely to build something meaningful with the right person.

There are many areas where boundaries matter. Some are practical, like time and money, while others are deeply personal, like values and emotional needs. Being aware of them from the start can prevent misunderstandings, resentment, and wasted effort.

Time and Energy

A new relationship can feel all-consuming, but no relationship should take over your life. It is easy to lose yourself in the excitement, spending all your free time with your partner and neglecting work, friendships, hobbies, and self-care. In the beginning, this might feel romantic, but over time, it can lead to imbalance and burnout.

A healthy relationship respects the balance between togetherness and individuality. If you find yourself constantly rearranging your schedule, dropping important commitments, or feeling guilty for taking time for yourself, that is a sign of an unhealthy dynamic. A good partner will understand that you have a life outside the relationship and will support your need for independence.

If someone expects you to be available at all times, becomes upset when you spend time apart or makes you feel guilty for maintaining your own interests, they are not respecting your time and energy. The most fulfilling relationships are those where both people have full and rewarding lives outside of each other.

Lifestyle Choices and Core Beliefs

Attraction alone cannot sustain a relationship. No matter how much chemistry you feel with someone, if your fundamental values and lifestyles do not align, problems will eventually arise. Religion and spirituality, for example, play a huge role in many people's lives. Whether you are deeply religious, atheist, or somewhere in between, being with a partner who does not share or at least respect your beliefs can lead to friction.

Diet and lifestyle choices also matter. A strict vegan may find it challenging to be with someone who eats meat regularly, just as someone who enjoys drinking socially may struggle with a partner who is strictly sober. Attitudes toward recreational drugs, political views, and LGBTQ+ issues can be similarly divisive. If you are an ally with close gay or lesbian friends, but your partner is uncomfortable with that, the tension will not disappear.

People do not change their core beliefs just because they are in love. If you ignore fundamental incompatibilities at the start, you cannot blame the other person when they later become a source of conflict. If you do not take lifestyle differences seriously, the heartbreak in the end will be your own fault.

Past Relationships and Contact with Exes

A healthy relationship does not require erasing the past, but it does require honesty and respect regarding previous relationships. If someone has children with an ex, ongoing communication is necessary, and any new partner must accept that reality. Similarly, some people maintain genuine platonic friendships with former partners. This is not necessarily a red flag as long as it is open, transparent, and respectful of the current relationship.

If a past relationship is truly over, there should be no secrecy. If a partner hides their contact with an ex, downplays the nature of their interactions, or reacts defensively when questioned, it may indicate unresolved emotions. Equally, if someone demands that you cut off all contact with your past, even when there is no valid reason, that is a sign of insecurity and control.

Family and Friendships

No one has the right to come into your life and dictate who you can and cannot associate with. If you have close friendships and strong family ties, a supportive partner will respect those relationships rather than try to isolate you.

That said, your partner should feel comfortable meeting the important people in your life, just as you should be able to meet theirs. If there are people in their life whom you are deliberately kept away from, or if your partner refuses to introduce you to close friends or family, that raises questions about transparency. In a healthy relationship, neither partner should have connections that the other cannot meet comfortably.

Sexual Boundaries

Sexual compatibility and mutual respect are essential in any intimate relationship. A healthy partnership allows both people to express their needs, preferences, and limits without fear of judgment, pressure, or coercion. Conversations about intimacy should be approached with honesty and mutual understanding. If you feel uncomfortable or uncertain, you have the absolute right to set limits and take things at your own pace.

A respectful partner will listen and adjust to your comfort level rather than guilt-trip or pressure you into anything. Any form of coercion, manipulation, or dismissal of your boundaries is unacceptable. It is also important to recognize that boundaries can change over time. What feels right in one stage of the relationship may shift as trust and connection grow. The key is that changes happen on your terms, not because you feel pressured to meet someone else's expectations.

Your body, your pace, and your choices are yours alone. No one should make you feel ashamed for maintaining your boundaries, and no one who truly cares for you will attempt to override them.

Financial Boundaries

Money can be a source of conflict in relationships, particularly if financial expectations are not discussed early. It is vital to establish clear boundaries around spending, sharing expenses, and financial responsibilities before any tensions arise.

A healthy relationship does not place financial burdens on one person, nor should there be an expectation of financial support, especially in the early stages. A partner who frequently asks for money, assumes you will pay for everything, or pressures you into financial commitments before trust has been built is showing a red flag. Similarly, a partner who is secretive about finances, avoids discussing shared financial responsibilities, or makes major purchases that affect both of you without discussion is not respecting financial boundaries.

Fairness is key. A balanced relationship involves financial responsibilities that are mutually agreed upon, taking into account individual circumstances, incomes, and shared expectations. Financial discussions may feel uncomfortable, but avoiding them can lead to resentment and an unhealthy dynamic where one person holds financial control over the other.

Emotional Boundaries and Personal Space

A healthy relationship provides emotional support, but it should not come at the expense of one person's well-being. If you find yourself constantly managing your partner's emotions, absorbing their stress, or feeling responsible for their happiness while your own needs are ignored, the relationship has become unbalanced.

Emotional support should be a two-way exchange, not a one-sided burden. If a partner expects you to carry their emotional weight but dismisses your struggles, it is a sign that they are not offering the same level of care and consideration that they demand. A strong relationship is built on mutual empathy, where both people feel heard, supported, and understood.

Similarly, personal space is essential. You do not owe anyone constant availability, and a partner who truly respects you will understand your need for solitude, independent interests, and friendships outside of the relationship. Time apart is not a sign of disinterest or detachment; it is a sign of a healthy and balanced connection.

A secure partner will never make you feel guilty for needing time alone, nor will they take offense when you prioritize self-care. Personal space strengthens a relationship by allowing each person to maintain their own identity and emotional well-being.

Digital Privacy and Social Media

In a world where so much of life is shared online, digital boundaries are just as important as personal ones. Social media and digital communication can create misunderstandings, stir up insecurities, and even be used as a tool for control if boundaries are not clearly defined.

Couples should make joint decisions about what is shared publicly, what remains private, and what level of digital involvement feels appropriate. A respectful partner will never post personal details about your relationship without discussing it first, nor will they expect unrestricted access to your phone, messages, or social media accounts. Trust does not require surveillance, and any demand for full transparency as a form of reassurance is an invasion of privacy.

If a partner becomes possessive over your social media activity, questions every interaction, or pressures you to delete certain friends or followers, they are crossing a boundary. Digital trust should be treated the same as real-world trust, built on respect and communication rather than control.

Boundaries in Disagreements and Conflict Resolution

Disagreements are inevitable in any relationship, but the way they are handled determines whether they strengthen or weaken the connection.

A disagreement should never turn into a personal attack. Name-calling, stonewalling, or withdrawing affection as a form of punishment are all signs of unhealthy conflict resolution.

A relationship should be a safe space where both people feel comfortable expressing concerns and emotions without fear of retaliation or silent resentment. If one partner consistently shuts down communication, avoids difficult conversations, or reacts with hostility instead of listening, it creates an environment where problems go unresolved, and emotions build up over time.

Boundaries in disagreements involve maintaining respect, listening actively, and working toward solutions rather than trying to "win" the argument. A healthy partner will approach conflict with a desire to understand and find common ground, not with an intention to dominate or belittle.

Guilt and Obligation as Boundary Violations

One of the most subtle and damaging ways boundaries are broken is through guilt and obligation. If a partner makes you feel guilty for asserting your needs, implies that setting boundaries means you do not love them or plays the victim when they do not get their way, they are manipulating you.

Guilt should never be used as a tool to control behavior. A partner who truly respects you will accept your boundaries without needing to make you feel bad about them. Healthy relationships allow for individual choices without the constant pressure to prove love through self-sacrifice.

If you feel obligated to stay in a relationship out of guilt rather than genuine desire, or if you fear that setting boundaries will cause emotional retaliation, it is a sign that your partner is not respecting your autonomy. A loving relationship allows both people to express their needs without fear of punishment or emotional blackmail.

Setting and Maintaining Boundaries

Setting boundaries takes practice, but they are essential for protecting yourself while fostering healthy connections. They create a foundation of respect in relationships and safeguard your emotional well-being. Boundaries are not about controlling others. They are about honoring yourself and ensuring that your needs and values are upheld. When set clearly and consistently, they help you build relationships that are based on trust, mutual understanding, and emotional safety.

Know What You Want

Before you can set boundaries, you need to understand what matters to you. Reflect on your personal needs, values, and non-negotiables. Consider what behaviors you find unacceptable, how you prefer to communicate, and how much time and energy you are willing to dedicate to a relationship.

Clarity in your own mind makes it easier to recognize when a boundary is being crossed. It also helps you communicate those boundaries effectively. Knowing your limits is not about being rigid or difficult. It is about ensuring that your relationships align with your personal well-being.

Communicate Clearly

Once you have identified your boundaries, you must communicate them openly and assertively. Many boundary violations occur not because someone is deliberately overstepping but because expectations were never clearly expressed.

Avoid vague language or expecting others to simply know what you need. Be direct but respectful. For example:

- "I value honesty, so if plans change, I would appreciate being informed rather than being left waiting."

- *"I prefer taking my time to get to know someone before rushing into commitments."*

When you express your needs clearly and calmly, you set the tone for mutual respect. A healthy partner will appreciate this clarity rather than feel threatened by it.

Pay Attention to Their Reactions

How someone responds to your boundaries tells you everything you need to know about their character. A respectful person will acknowledge and appreciate your clarity, even if they do not always agree. They may ask questions or seek to understand your perspective, but they will not push back in a way that feels dismissive or manipulative.

A toxic or emotionally immature person may test, dismiss, or guilt-trip you for asserting your needs. They might accuse you of being too sensitive, controlling, or unreasonable. Trust your instincts if their reaction makes you feel uneasy. Words can be misleading, but consistent patterns of behavior reveal a person's true nature.

Enforce Your Boundaries

Setting boundaries is only half the battle. You also need to uphold them. If someone crosses a line, calmly restate your boundary and introduce consequences if necessary. If a new friend repeatedly cancels plans at the last minute, you might say, *"I value my time, so if plans keep getting canceled, I will need to reconsider making future arrangements."*

Consistency is key. If you allow repeated violations, you unintentionally communicate that your boundaries are flexible or unimportant. People who are used to getting their way may continue to test your limits, hoping you will eventually give in. If this happens, stand firm. You are not responsible for their discomfort in response to your boundaries.

Recognize When to Walk Away

Some people will never respect your boundaries, no matter how clearly you communicate them. If someone consistently disregards your needs, dismisses your concerns, or makes you feel guilty for setting limits, it is a sign that they do not truly value you or the relationship.

Leaving a situation where your boundaries are repeatedly ignored is not a failure. It is an act of self-respect. Staying in an environment that erodes your self-worth will only cause long-term damage. Walking away creates space for healthier, more supportive connections where your needs are met and your boundaries are honored.

Trust Your Instincts

The most important tool in boundary-setting is trusting your instincts. If something feels off, do not ignore that feeling. Your gut reaction is often more accurate than the justifications you create in your mind. If someone continuously pushes past your comfort zone, minimizes your feelings, or makes you feel guilty for standing up for yourself, it is a red flag.

A strong and healthy relationship is one where both people feel safe, valued, and understood. Boundaries are not just about preventing toxic relationships. They are also about ensuring that the right relationships thrive. When two people respect each other's limits and communicate openly, trust and connection naturally deepen.

The next chapter explores what a truly healthy relationship looks like, how to recognize one, and how to build a connection that is based on mutual respect, trust, and emotional security.

9

Building Healthy Relationships

Dating is one of life's great adventures. It is a chance to connect, laugh, explore new experiences, and learn more about yourself along the way. While there may be moments of uncertainty, most of the time, dating is exciting and full of potential. Each new interaction holds the possibility of something wonderful, whether it is a short-lived romance that adds joy to your life or the start of something deeper and long-lasting.

The key to navigating dating successfully is awareness. It is not about fearing what could go wrong but about recognizing what makes a relationship right. Understanding the qualities of a healthy relationship allows you to move forward with confidence, knowing you are communicating with prospective partners who can contribute to your happiness rather than detract from it.

A great relationship is not about perfection. It is about partnership. A fulfilling connection is built on mutual respect, trust, and the shared goal of growing together. Even if you have had difficult experiences in the past, this chapter is a hopeful reminder that genuine, meaningful relationships are absolutely within reach.

What Healthy Relationships Look Like

Healthy relationships create an environment where both partners feel valued, heard, and supported. They offer emotional safety, encourage personal growth, and allow each person to thrive both individually and together. While no relationship is without challenges, certain qualities and dynamics consistently appear in strong, lasting connections. Here are some of those attributes:

Mutual Respect

Respect is the foundation of any healthy relationship. It means valuing each other's perspectives, listening without judgment, and treating one another as equals. In a relationship based on respect, both partners feel safe to express themselves, knowing their opinions, emotions, and boundaries will be honored.

Mutual respect also includes celebrating each other's achievements, supporting individual goals, and recognizing that a relationship is not about control or dominance. When both people feel equally valued, the connection deepens, and the relationship flourishes.

Honest And Open Communication

Clear, open communication is the key to resolving misunderstandings, strengthening trust, and deepening emotional intimacy. A healthy partner is willing to talk about concerns constructively rather than resorting to blame, manipulation, or defensiveness.

In a strong relationship, both partners can express their needs and vulnerabilities without fear of judgment. They listen to one another with the intent to understand, not just to respond. Difficult conversations are approached with patience, and disagreements are handled with a focus on resolution rather than winning. When communication is honest and respectful, a relationship becomes a place of security and connection.

Consistency and Reliability

Trust is built through consistency. A reliable partner follows through on their commitments, keeps their word, and behaves in a way that aligns with their actions. Reliability is not just about remembering dates or showing up on time. It is about being emotionally steady and present in the relationship.

A trustworthy partner does not create confusion about their intentions. Their actions match their words, and they do not play emotional games. Knowing you can depend on your partner provides a deep sense of security, which allows the relationship to grow without uncertainty or doubt.

Emotional Safety

In a healthy relationship, you can be your true self without fear of criticism, ridicule, or rejection. Emotional safety means feeling secure enough to express your joys, fears, and struggles, knowing your partner will respond with care and understanding.

A strong relationship allows for vulnerability. Both partners should be able to share their emotions without worrying that they will be dismissed or used against them. Conflict is handled with respect, where both people feel heard, and disagreements do not turn into personal attacks.

Shared Values and Life Goals

Differences can add richness to a relationship, but alignment in key values provides stability. Significant aspects of life, such as views on family, lifestyle, career ambitions, and personal growth, should be openly discussed early on.

If one person dreams of a quiet life in the countryside while the other envisions a fast-paced city existence, or if one values financial security while the other prioritizes spontaneity and adventure, these differences may create friction over time. Recognizing these potential conflicts early on allows for honest conversations about whether long-term compatibility is realistic.

Common Interests and Support for Individual Passions

Sharing interests provides opportunities for connection and fun. Whether it is music, hiking, cooking, or travel, engaging in activities together strengthens the bond between partners.

At the same time, a healthy relationship respects and encourages individuality. You do not need to do everything together, and it is just as important to have hobbies and passions that your partner supports but does not necessarily participate in. Respecting personal interests fosters independence within the relationship, reinforcing that you are two complete individuals choosing to share a life rather than becoming dependent on one another.

Comfort and Transparency in Relationships with Others

Neither partner should have anyone in their life that they cannot comfortably introduce to the other. Whether it is a long-term friend, an ex, or a colleague, transparency about external relationships is important. If someone feels the need to hide or downplay a connection, it creates unnecessary tension and erodes trust.

Similarly, if you meet someone in your partner's life and find the dynamic uncomfortable, it is worth discussing why. A healthy partner will listen to and address concerns openly rather than becoming defensive or dismissive.

Staying Hopeful and Empowered

Dating is meant to be enjoyable. Even when setbacks occur, they are learning experiences that bring you closer to finding what you truly want in a partner. Each new interaction teaches you more about your own values, preferences, and boundaries.

If you are starting a new relationship, focus on what makes it exciting. Enjoy the process of getting to know someone while remaining mindful of what you have learned about red flags and healthy relationship dynamics. Trust in your ability to make choices that prioritize your happiness and well-being.

For those healing from past relationships, take comfort in knowing that recovery is possible. The lessons learned from past experiences will guide you toward a better future. Building a healthy relationship is not just about finding the right person. It is about becoming the best version of yourself, one who recognizes and nurtures genuine love.

Moving Forward

A healthy relationship is built on mutual respect, shared values, and the desire to grow together. It allows you to be your authentic self while supporting your partner's journey as well. As you move forward, trust in your ability to create connections that inspire, uplift, and empower you.

Dating is not about finding someone to complete you. It is about finding someone who complements the life you are already building. By staying true to your values, trusting your instincts, and embracing your worth, you are setting the stage for a future filled with meaningful, fulfilling relationships.

10

Moving Forward with Confidence

Dating and relationships should be a journey of discovery, growth, and joy. While there are risks and challenges, especially in today's fast-paced world of online dating, awareness allows you to navigate these experiences with confidence. The purpose of this book has not been to instill fear or suspicion but to equip you with the tools to recognize healthy connections and protect yourself from unhealthy ones.

Awareness is your greatest ally. It helps you trust your instincts, set boundaries, and recognize when a relationship is truly serving your happiness and well-being. Whether you have experienced toxic relationships in the past or are stepping into the dating world for the first time, the knowledge you have gained here is a robust foundation. You now have the ability to recognize patterns of behavior, assess whether a relationship is fulfilling or draining, and, most importantly, take action when necessary.

Empowerment Through Awareness

Awareness is not about overanalyzing or second-guessing every interaction. It is about staying present and recognizing what aligns with your values and emotional health. In the fast-moving world of dating, where charm and attraction can sometimes mask deeper issues, your ability to discern genuine connections is crucial. Recognizing early warning signs such as manipulation, inconsistent behavior, or a lack of respect for your boundaries allows you to make decisions that protect your emotional well-being.

For those in the early stages of a relationship, awareness helps you assess whether your needs are being met. Are you feeling heard and respected? Is there a balance in how affection and attention are shared? Are you excited about the connection, or are you constantly questioning where you stand? Awareness is about staying grounded and ensuring that the relationship brings out the best in you.

The Role of Boundaries

Boundaries are the foundation of healthy relationships. They create space for trust, respect, and emotional security, ensuring that both partners feel valued and supported. Setting and maintaining boundaries is not about pushing people away. It is about defining what is acceptable and ensuring that your needs are honored without compromising your self-respect.

In dating, boundaries help filter out individuals who are not aligned with your values or emotional well-being. If someone consistently pushes your limits, disregards your feelings, or makes you feel guilty for asserting your needs, they are showing you who they are. Paying attention to these behaviors early on can save you from months or even years of frustration.

Boundaries also prevent you from losing yourself in a relationship. They remind you that your identity is not defined by your partner but by your own values, passions, and goals. Learning to set and uphold boundaries is not just a skill for dating. It is a life skill that improves every relationship, from romantic partnerships to friendships and professional interactions.

From Awareness to Action

Recognizing problematic behaviors is only the first step. True empowerment comes from taking action to protect yourself and prioritize your well-being. Whether that means stepping away from a connection that does not feel right or embracing one that aligns with your values, the choice is ultimately yours.

Remember the guideline: once is unfortunate, twice is a coincidence, and three times is a pattern. Patterns do not lie. They offer clarity in assessing whether a relationship is worth pursuing or if it is slowly eroding your emotional health. If someone repeatedly disrespects your boundaries, dismisses your feelings, or makes you question your own worth, it is time to walk away.

Taking action also means trusting yourself. If something feels off, do not dismiss it. Reflect on why you feel uneasy and allow that awareness to guide your decisions. Action is not about being reactive or confrontational. It is about being intentional and making choices that align with your emotional health and future happiness.

Staying Hopeful

Dating should be an exciting and fulfilling experience. While setbacks and disappointments may happen, they are not signs that love is out of reach. Every interaction teaches you something about yourself: what you value, what you need, and what kind of connection will genuinely complement your life.

Even if you have had toxic experiences in the past, they do not define your future. Healing takes time, but it is possible. The lessons you have learned will guide you toward stronger, healthier relationships. Each step you take toward prioritizing your emotional health brings you closer to the kind of love you deserve.

The joy of dating lies in possibility. It is about meeting new people, sharing experiences, and discovering what truly makes you happy. When approached with awareness and confidence, dating is not just about avoiding harm. It is about embracing the excitement of finding someone who brings out the best in you and who celebrates who you are.

A Journey Worth Taking

At its core, this book is about empowerment. It is about equipping you to approach dating and relationships with self-respect, confidence, and hope. You deserve a relationship that uplifts, respects, and helps you grow.

Healthy relationships are not without challenges, but they are built on mutual care, understanding, and a shared commitment to creating something meaningful. With the insights you have gained, you are better prepared to recognize those relationships and avoid the ones that could harm your well-being.

As you move forward, trust yourself. Trust that you can recognize healthy dynamics. Trust that your boundaries matter. Trust that you are worthy of safe, supportive, and fulfilling love.

Thank you for taking this journey. May the knowledge and confidence you have gained guide you toward the connections you deserve and the happiness you seek.

11

Reference

American Psychiatric Association (2013) *Diagnostic and statistical manual of mental disorders: DSM-5.* 5th ed. Washington, D.C.: American Psychiatric Publishing.

III

BONUS CHAPTER

Long Distance Relationships

12

The Special Case of Long-Distance Relationships

Long-distance relationships are a special case. Unlike traditional relationships where partners live in the same city or region, long-distance relationships present unique challenges that require a higher level of intentionality, communication, and long-term planning. While they can be fulfilling, they also demand a realistic and well-thought-out strategy to ensure they are not just an emotional investment with no real future.

The excitement of connecting with someone far away can initially feel romantic and adventurous. The anticipation of visits, long conversations, and the extra effort involved in staying in touch can make the relationship feel meaningful and even more intense than a local one. However, without a clear pathway toward eventually living in the same place, these relationships often lead to frustration and heartache. No long-distance relationship should be sustained indefinitely without progress toward closing the physical distance.

The Question of Relocation

One of the hardest but most necessary discussions in a long-distance relationship is about relocation. If neither person is willing to move, then the relationship has no real future. This is a difficult conversation, but it must happen early. It is not enough to say, *"We will figure it out later."* Avoiding this discussion does not change the reality that, at some point, a decision must be made.

Both people need to be honest about their willingness and ability to relocate. Career opportunities, family obligations, financial stability, and social support systems all factor into the decision. If one person has children from a previous relationship, moving may not even be an option. Relocation is not just about logistics. It is a major life decision that requires a realistic discussion of sacrifices and expectations.

Moving away from one's home means leaving behind friends, family, work connections, and familiar surroundings. If one person relocates, the adjustment period can be challenging. Resentment can build if they feel unsupported or if expectations were not properly discussed beforehand. This is why it is essential to weigh the full impact of relocation before making promises that might later feel impossible to keep.

Communication and Managing Expectations

Communication is the foundation of any long-distance relationship, but expectations must be clearly defined. Without clear boundaries, misunderstandings can arise, leading to disappointment and emotional strain.

- **How often will you communicate?** One person may expect daily phone calls and video chats, while the other prefers more occasional check-ins. If expectations are mismatched, frustration and feelings of neglect can develop.
- **How often will you visit?** Unlike in-person relationships, where

spontaneous meetups are possible, long-distance couples must plan their time together in advance. Who will travel more often? How frequently will visits happen? What happens if travel becomes difficult due to financial constraints, work schedules, or unforeseen circumstances? If only one person is making an effort to visit while the other is not reciprocating, resentment will inevitably build.

- **What are the boundaries around exclusivity?** Assumptions about commitment can be dangerous in a long-distance relationship. While one person may assume exclusivity, the other may see the situation as more flexible. If this is not openly discussed, it can lead to deep hurt and betrayal. It is essential to clarify early on whether the relationship is exclusive and what both people expect in terms of commitment.

The Illusion of Perfection and the Slow Process of Truly Knowing Someone

One of the biggest challenges in long-distance relationships is that partners inevitably spend far less in-person time together than couples who live in the same city. This means that you do not see how the other person behaves in everyday life, how they handle stress, or how they interact with people outside of romantic moments. Because time together is limited, when they do meet up, both partners tend to be on their best behavior, making every visit feel exciting and fulfilling.

Since visits are short and precious, there is a tendency to focus on making them enjoyable rather than addressing serious topics. Conversations about life goals, financial expectations, or fundamental compatibility issues can get postponed because bringing them up feels like ruining the little time you have together. Over time, this avoidance can create a false sense of security in the relationship. Everything seems perfect during visits, but the deeper challenges remain unaddressed. The longer this continues, the more time is lost.

It can take months, or even years, to truly see the full picture of someone that you are seeing in a long-distance relationship. This is not because either person is being dishonest, but simply because the relationship lacks the natural day-to-day interactions that reveal how someone handles real-life stress, financial decisions, social interactions, and personal habits. If a long-distance couple eventually moves in together, they may find that they are much less compatible than they assumed because they never had the opportunity to observe each other continuously in a normal, everyday setting.

The Risk of Wasting Time

One of the biggest dangers of a long-distance relationship is investing months or years into something that ultimately has no future. If a couple is not actively working toward being in the same place, then the relationship is little more than an emotional distraction. While love and connection are important, they are not enough on their own.

For a long-distance relationship to work, both partners must be proactive and committed to finding solutions together. It is not enough for one person to always be the one making the effort. There must be a shared responsibility, a willingness to compromise, and a genuine desire to make the relationship work beyond just words.

If, after honest discussions, it becomes clear that the logistical and emotional challenges outweigh the potential for a real future together, it is better to recognize that early rather than investing years in something that has no viable long-term outcome.

Final Thoughts

Long-distance relationships are not inherently doomed to fail, but they require more planning, communication, and long-term vision than traditional relationships. Without a clear plan for how and when the distance will eventually be closed, they often lead to emotional exhaustion and disappointment.

A successful long-distance relationship is built on honesty, intentional effort, and shared goals. If those elements are missing, it is important to ask whether the relationship is truly worth the sacrifice. If neither person is willing or able to take the necessary steps to be together in the same place, then it is not really a relationship. It is a long, drawn-out goodbye.